IV

Learning from Nature

Learning from Nature

Cross-Curricular Activities to Foster Creative and Critical Thinking

Robert Myers

Zephyr Press

Chicago

Library of Congress Cataloging-in-Publication Data
Myers, R. E.
    Learning from nature : cross-curricular activities to foster creative and
    critical thinking / R. E. Myers.— 1st ed.
    p. cm.
    Includes bibliographical references and index.
    ISBN 1-56976-194-9
    1. Nature study—Activity programs—United States. 2. Interdisciplinary
    approach in education—United States. 3. Critical thinking—Study and
    teaching (Elementary)—United States. I. Title.
    LB1585.3.M94 2005
    372.35′7′044—dc22   2004030257

Cover design: Scott Rattray/Rattray Design
Cover photo: Daniel Bosler/TSW

Published by Zephyr Press
An imprint of Chicago Review Press, Incorporated
814 North Franklin Street
Chicago, Illinois 60610
ISBN 1-56976-194-9
Printed in the United States of America

This book is dedicated to Fritz and Lynne Reeker
with great admiration and gratitude.

What is life? It is the flash of a firefly in the night. It is the breath of a buffalo in the wintertime. It is the little shadow, which runs across the grass and loses itself in the sunset.

—Crowfoot

Contents

Curricular Tie-Ins

Unit Title	Drawing	Language Arts	Mathematics	Music	Science	Social Studies
Jan's Bug		•			•	
The Biggest Ruby of All		•			•	
Six-Legged Friends		•			•	
Abel		•			•	
In Balance	•	•	•			•
Mervin's Mess		•			•	
There's Chew (The Chow)		•			•	
Holes	•				•	•
Dogs		•				•
Animal Talk		•			•	
Funny Bunnies		•			•	
Which Doesn't Fit?					•	•
Quakes		•			•	•
To Catch a Frog	•	•				
Water	•	•			•	
At the Bottom of the Sea		•			•	
Fished Out		•			•	•
Catching a Water Beetle		•			•	
Nan Meets a Bird	•	•			•	•
Just Like a Crow		•			•	
Sing Like the Birds		•		•	•	
A January Mystery		•			•	
A Lot of Air		•			•	
Smoke		•			•	
Fog		•			•	
Like a Balloon	•	•			•	
Jacks in Space		•			•	

Curricular Tie-Ins (Continued)

Unit Title	Drawing	Language Arts	Mathematics	Music	Science	Social Studies
Bubbles	●	●			●	
Sky Watch		●			●	
It's Hot!		●			●	
Floating Round	●	●			●	
Come Back		●			●	
More Than Music		●		●	●	
Waking Up		●			●	●
Would You Rather Be a Mouse?		●			●	●
You Can't See Me		●			●	
Kings and Queens		●			●	
Pinecone or Orchid	●	●			●	
In Your Hands		●			●	
Riding a Sunbeam		●			●	
Just Dreaming	●	●			●	
Your Favorite Things		●			●	●
Mixing		●			●	●
Fly, Fly		●			●	
Sing While You Work	●	●		●	●	
Three	●	●			●	●
Four		●			●	
Seasons		●			●	●
What Is the Best Time?		●			●	●
Afraid?		●			●	●
What Comes Next?			●		●	●
Where Have You Seen This Before?	●	●			●	●
For a Better World		●			●	●

Introduction

This book is designed to encourage children to think more deeply about the world in which they live. The activities relate to nature and the everyday lives of young people, and emphasize those creative and critical thinking skills that children in primary grades benefit most from using and developing. What do we mean by "thinking skills"? There are many ways to describe how individuals think, but we have chosen to categorize thinking into 21 skills. A list of these thinking skills appears on page xviii. The creative thinking skills are those named by E. Paul Torrance in his Incubation Model of Teaching.

We hope that your students will give more than just a quick thought to the questions posed in the activities. Encourage them to reflect on each question before going to the next one. Some children believe that getting through an activity quickly is their first priority. Although some school activities reward speed as an indication of efficiency and proficiency, speed shouldn't be a goal for any of the activities in *Learning from Nature*.

It is both sound pedagogical practice and good common sense to modify materials to fit the characteristics, backgrounds, and interests of your students. Please change any of the activities as you see fit and skip over any that don't seem suitable for your students or your program.

After Howard Gardner designated "Naturalist" as his eighth multiple intelligence, schools had an added impetus to emphasize a learning approach that is familiar to young people. Some children enjoy catching and mounting insects; others like to collect leaves; and yet others are eager to capture and keep all manner of animals. Some children are fascinated by the variety in nature and learn to name and classify plants and animals. This interest in the natural world should be fostered in the primary grades and used as a springboard for investigating the phenomena found in the everyday lives of children.

Learning from Nature deals with a wide variety of topics—the weather, mammals, birds, insects, the earth, seasons, the sky, and the ocean—and provides excellent starter activities for any number of science units in your curriculum. Its creative thinking element lets children relate to the topics personally and unself-consciously. Each lesson calls for one or more creative thinking skills.

Your students should respond to *Learning from Nature* by both thinking and doing. The lessons are designed to provoke thought and the students' desire to dig deeper into the topics introduced. Whether it is finding out more about the stars and planets or the behavior of blackbirds and crows, the student should be motivated to extend his or her knowledge of nature by these lessons.

Thinking Skills

These are the critical and creative thinking skills called for in the activities in *Learning from Nature*. These symbols can be found at the bottom of the first page of each activity.

Abbreviation	Meaning
AE	Being Aware of Emotions
AN	Analyzing
BT	Breaking Through/Extending Boundaries
CS	Combining and Synthesizing
E	Elaborating
EF	Enjoying and Using Fantasy
F	Being Flexible
H	Letting Humor Flow
HE	Highlighting the Essence
HY	Hypothesizing
JU	Judging
KO	Keeping Open
LAW	Looking at It in Another Way
O	Being Original
OF	Orienting to the Future
PA	Producing Alternatives
PIC	Putting Ideas into Context
S	Being Sensitive/Finding the Problem
SR	Making It Swing, Making It Ring
VI	Visualizing Inside
VRC	Visualizing Richly and Colorfully

Learning from Nature

Unit 1

Jan's Bug

Setting the Stage for the Unit

Consider using this unit early in the school year, because it focuses students' attention on seeking out information. Jan's Bug is a very short story about a youngster who wants to identify a bug. You might lead into the lesson by asking your students if they ever wonder about the names of plants or creatures, or if they have questions about such matters as why the dead bodies of rabbits or squirrels aren't seen very often. Do they wonder about what the name of a pretty bird or funny-looking insect is? Are there children in the class who have books in their homes about flowers, birds, or trees?

Administering the Unit

Some of the activities that can be used with this unit are:

Developing the Naturalistic and Verbal-Linguistic Intelligences

The idea of the unit is to encourage students to be curious about natural phenomena and to point out that there are several ways to obtain information about things in nature. You can record on the chalkboard the ways that information can be obtained.

Often it is important to know which insects are beneficial and which are harmful. Encourage the students who know about insects to share their knowledge. One or two may be able to distinguish the help-ful ladybug from the diabolical Diabrotica beetle, for instance.

Developing the Mathematical-Logical Intelligence

If your students haven't been introduced to a rudimentary taxonomy of living things, you might use this unit to explain distinctions that scientists make about differentiating among species. There are a tremendous number of beetles, for example.

Developing the Visual-Spatial Intelligence

Your students will probably enjoy drawing their ideas about what Jan's bug is like. This isn't an opportunity for them to draw wild, unrealistic creatures, however. Their conceptions should be based on reality. For more information, they can consult reference books for their drawings. Here are some books you might find helpful: *Insectigations: 40 Hands-on Activities to Explore the Insect World* (Chicago Review Press, 2005), *Bugs Are Insects* (HarperCollins, 2001), and National Audubon Society *First Field Guide: Insects* (Scholastic, 1998).

Following Through

Because there promises to be a good deal of variety in your students' drawings, it might be entertaining to display them on a bulletin board. Children always enjoy seeing their work displayed, as all primary teachers know.

Jan's Bug

Jan saw a bug in her yard. She thought it could be a beetle. It had a long, black body and orange spots on its sides. The bug also had very long "feelers."

Jan picked up the bug, carefully. She went to her mother and showed her the bug. Jan's mother didn't know the name of the bug. There wasn't a book in the house about bugs. Since it was Sunday, Jan couldn't go to a library. But she wanted to find out about the bug.

What could Jan do to find out about the bug?

_____

_____

_____

_____

_____

_____

_____

_____

_____

The Biggest Ruby of All

Setting the Stage for the Unit

This unit is designed to extend your students' thinking by requiring them to come up with interesting questions. A good way to warm them up for this lesson is to make the connection between rubies and jewelry. Ask if any of them has ever found a ring, a bracelet, or a precious stone. There's a good possibility one of them has.

Administering the Unit

Some activities that can be used in tandem with The Biggest Ruby of All include:

Developing the Naturalistic Intelligence

The unit should stir up some interest in gems. Many of the larger dictionaries have illustrations of gemstones, including, of course, the ruby. Encyclopedias have fascinating articles about gemstones and are an additional source of illustrations. The fascination with precious stones and pearls is nearly universal, so you might encourage your students to explore the subject in more detail.

Developing the Verbal-Linguistic Intelligence

In recent years, educators have focused on helping students improve their ability to ask questions that will provide interesting and valuable information. Nancy Johnson's *Active Questioning* (Pieces of Learning, 1995), for example, talks about developing questioning skills. Ask your students to pose questions to the owner of "the world's largest ruby." You can also ask them to come up with hypothetical questions for a professional juggler, a person who has never watched television, a clown who entertains at birthday parties, a mountain climber who has reached the summits of all the world's highest peaks, or other remarkable people. If one of your students

has a rock collection, he or she would probably be pleased to show it to the class and answer their questions about it. To develop your students' questioning skills further, encourage them to ask interesting local people questions, when appropriate.

Developing Visual-Spatial Skills

The structure of crystals can be very complex. Drawing the most detailed facets of a ruby is probably too difficult for your students, but they can explore rubies' various colorations and learn how the brilliance of gems is measured. (A gem's index of refraction accurately measures its luster.) Good children's books about crystals, rocks, and precious stones are available in most libraries. Here are some you might find helpful: *Crystal and Gem* (Alfred Knopf, 1991) and *Crystals and Crystal Gardens You Can Grow* (Franklin Watts, 1990).

> ## Rubies
>
> *A ruby is the red gem variety of the mineral called corundum (aluminum oxide). Large rubies are the rarest and costliest of gems. Not all rubies are exactly the same color. Some are pink and some are almost brown. Corundums that aren't red are usually called sapphires.*

Following Through

If it is feasible and The Biggest Ruby of All generates enough interest, a specialist in gems might be invited to class. Jewelers are often enthusiastic about their business, and one in your community may very well be willing to come to school to talk about gems.

Unit 2

The Biggest Ruby of All

Gems are stones used to make jewelry. The ruby is a very rare gem. Its color is usually red. A very large ruby may be worth more than a diamond. The best rubies are found in Burma.

Suppose that your teacher knows the man who has found the biggest ruby in the world and invites him to come to your class. So that everyone won't talk at once, your teacher asks Stan to ask the first three questions of the man. With the help of the class, Stan decides upon these three questions:

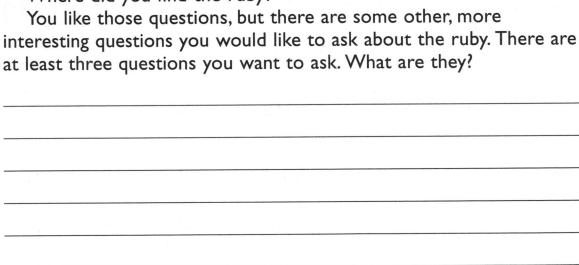

How big is the ruby you found?

How much is it worth?

Where did you find the ruby?

You like those questions, but there are some other, more interesting questions you would like to ask about the ruby. There are at least three questions you want to ask. What are they?

_____

_____

_____

_____

_____

_____

Learning from Nature © 2005 • www.zephyrpress.com

Unit 3

Six-Legged Friends

Setting the Stage for the Unit

This unit is about Sam's love of insects. Except for flies, Sam was crazy about insects. Luckily for Sam, the world is heavily populated with insects. They are undoubtedly the most successful of all living organisms on earth, including dandelions. The more harmful insects are astounding in their ability to resist our attempts to eradicate them. As a class, these animals are amazingly diversified—scientists believe that from one million to ten million species have yet to be discovered. To introduce the unit, you can simply point out the insects that regularly invade the school and the homes of your students. Your room may have one or more of these guests—a moth, some ants, a fly, a mosquito or two, lice (hopefully not!), some fruit flies, among other possibilities. If you can find any of these insects and point them out to your class, it will provide an excellent lead-in to this story about a boy who was convinced that insects aren't all bad.

Administering the Unit

These are a few of the ways that Six-Legged Friends can be used to encourage the development of your students' multiple intelligences:

Developing the Naturalistic Intelligence

The idea of the story is that insects can be beneficial to people. They pollinate our crops, produce honey and other kinds of food (some primitive peoples depend on insects for sustenance), provide food for the animals we eat, and provide bait for people who fish. Insects are valuable to us in other ways, too. For example, we get pleasure from seeing and collecting those that are beautiful, such as butterflies and moths. Sam could only name one way that insects help us, but perhaps some of your students can mention these other ways. A good answer to the question

of what the earth would be like without insects is that life would certainly not be the same for us if there were no insects.

Developing the Verbal-Linguistic and the Mathematical-Logical Intelligences

If there are any students who take Sam's position in the argument about the desirability of insects, you can conduct a not-so-formal debate representing the two views expressed in the story. The students who are apt to weigh things impartially will grasp the fact that the good that insects do for mankind in pollinating plants more than offsets the damage they do (including the spreading of deadly diseases such as malaria).

Developing the Visual-Spatial Intelligence

It should help all of your students, and especially those who learn best through the visual modality, to have them draw an insect with its three parts and antennae. They can select a grasshopper or a cricket and show the spiracles through which the insect breathes, its wings, its compound eyes, and its mouth parts.

Following Through

If any of your students collect butterflies, moths, or beetles, encourage them to bring their collections to class so that the children can better appreciate the beauty and variety of insects. Children occasionally also keep crickets and other single insects in small boxes and other containers, and these can also be brought to class.

In the event none of your students is a collector of insects, there are many books, films, videos, and study prints about insects such as the monarch butterfly. Because of its dramatic metamorphosis and long-range migrations, the monarch butterfly is a particularly good insect to study.

Six-Legged Friends

Sam loved insects. He loved every kind of insect, even wasps and cockroaches. But he didn't like flies.

One day in class the children were talking about insects. Russ said that insects hurt people. Bees sting people. Grasshoppers eat plants. Mosquitoes bite us. Termites hurt houses. Even the larvae of butterflies eat vegetables.

Sam didn't like to hear that insects were bad. His best pet was a cricket that he named Happy. Sam told Russ that only one out of a hundred insects is bad for people. "Many help people," Sam said. He talked about the insects that allow flowers to form seeds. "A lot of plants couldn't make more plants like themselves without the help of insects," Sam said.

Several children then said that they still didn't like bees stinging them and ants coming into their houses. What else do insects do to help people, they wanted to know. Sam was stuck. He knew that he had explained only one way insects help people, but he couldn't think of more ways. He hadn't said enough to convince the others.

What are the other ways that insects help people? Name at least three.

_____

_____

_____

What would happen if there were no insects on earth?

_____

_____

_____

_____

_____

Unit 4

Abel

Setting the Stage for the Unit

If your classroom is located near a lawn or field of grass, all you need to do to introduce this unit is ask your students what they see out of the window. If you aren't lucky enough to have grass growing outside of your classroom, bringing a tuft of grass to the room and holding it up for identification will initiate the unit nicely. Grass is perhaps the most important living thing on earth!

Administering the Unit

A few of the activities that might accompany Abel are:

Developing the Naturalistic Intelligence

It would be hard to imagine what life would be like in the United States if there were no grasses, and the more reflective students will quickly grasp this notion. One of the great virtues of grass is that it is an extremely important food for wild and domesticated animals. What would we do without the meat we get from grazing animals? Of course, humans eat the grains of grasses, the cereals. It's hard to imagine children at the breakfast table without cereal, or their parents without bread. All green plants (including grass) produce sugar. However, most of the sugar we eat comes from a grass called sugar cane (the rest comes from sugar beets). Paper can also be made from grass. In addition, it is vital in saving the topsoil from erosion.

Developing Visual-Spatial Skills

Have your students sketch the principal parts of a grass plant so that they can appreciate that there is more to grass than the blades they see. There are also the roots, stems (culms), and flowers. Each leaf is made up of a sheath, blade, ligule, and collar. Grass stems are jointed, that is, made up of nodes.

Developing Verbal-Linguistic Skills

A number of excellent books written for children give the story of the grains. You may have one or more in your library. If a child is able to read one of these books, he or she can share the information with the class.

Following Through

If your pupils become interested in the various grasses and their immense importance to animals and people, a natural follow-up activity would be to have them bring to class examples of both unprocessed and processed grains. For example, in addition to lawn grass, a specimen of oats or rice might be brought in, and their processed versions—perhaps toasted oats and puffed rice cereal, in their boxes—could be displayed alongside them. The process that converts the live plants into breakfast foods is probably too complex for your pupils to readily grasp, but if there is genuine interest, there are reference materials (pamphlets, books, videos, and films) to delve into. *Cereal, Nuts, and Spices* (Silver Burdett, 1997) is an excellent source of information.

> ### Grass
>
> *Grass is one of the largest and most diverse families of plants. It can be found on all of the earth's land surfaces. Grasses can be short, like those used for lawns, or large and woody, like bamboo. They are both annual and perennial and can be further classified in six groups: (1) grazing and forage, (2) turf grasses, (3) ornamental grasses, (4) cereals, (5) sugar cane, and (6) woody grasses such as bamboo.*

Abel

Abel was an average boy of nine. He liked to play games, and he liked to ride his bike. In one way, though, Abel was a little different from his friends. He was clumsy. When he played soccer on the dirt fields, he would come home with bloody arms and legs. If he could, he always tried to play on the city's grass fields.

One day Abel started to think about why grass grows everywhere. He had just taken it for granted that grass seems to grow wherever there is dirt. But he began thinking more about why grass grows when he saw his father put some grass seeds on a bare patch in their lawn.

Now, Abel knew that plants grew from seed, but he hadn't thought of grass sprouting and growing that way. It was just *there*. Grass was softer than dirt and rocks, and it was nice to see lawns of green grass. He hadn't realized that sometimes people had to plant seeds to make it grow.

Besides giving us comfort and beauty, what other uses does grass have for people?

_____

_____

_____

_____

In Balance

Setting the Stage for the Unit

Although the illustration of the unicyclist sets the stage quite well for this unit about balance, you could also perform a little balancing act before the unit is handed out. The simplest, if you can manage it, is to balance a ruler or yardstick on your forefinger. Depending upon your skills, you might also balance one object on another to get your students in the proper frame of mind for thinking about this basic concept.

Administering the Unit

A few of the activities that can accompany this lesson are:

Developing the Mathematical-Logical Intelligence

The concept of balance is fundamentally about the relationship of physical objects, but it is applicable to nearly every aspect of life. Students who grasp that might put it into words (orally or on paper). Balance appeals to their sense of order. For those who understand balance to be mostly a physical condition, the unit begins with the example of the balance needed by a unicyclist (or trapeze artist, tightrope walker, juggler, circus performer standing on a horse, etc.). Your students have also been exposed to the concept of balance in arithmetic. If you ask them about it, students with logical minds will readily respond with algorithms and equations. They may even note balance in geometric figures, such as squares and triangles.

Developing the Bodily-Kinesthetic Intelligence

Students who are athletic will extend the idea of balance for the unicyclist to that required to ride a bicycle, skate, play on a teeter-totter, play football and basketball, play hopscotch, or even dance. Balance is basic to all athletic endeavors.

Developing the Visual-Spatial Intelligence

Ask students to draw a picture of something on the playground that requires balance or shows symmetry. The obvious choice is the teeter-totter. Almost any other piece of playground equipment or a game such as hopscotch will also work as an example.

Talking about balance in a picture may be a little advanced for your students, but a talented and/or perceptive individual will seize the opportunity to express his or her ideas about balance or symmetry in the visual arts.

Developing the Verbal-Linguistic Intelligence

Finding the correct words to describe matters of physics and aesthetics should prove challenging to your students. Those youngsters who have an advanced vocabulary will have a chance to describe situations and operations not usually encountered outside science units.

Developing the Interpersonal Intelligence

The question about balance in conversation should bring forth some interesting reactions. It is possible that the more verbal students will not be aware that their conversations with friends are often one-sided. It could come as a surprise to them that they dominate discussions and conversations.

Following Through

A number of extensions for this unit should come easily, if there is time for them. Although it could be too advanced for your class, you can ask about balance in music, architecture, and writing. Your students might have heard of balancing a checkbook or "balancing the books." The concept is basic to almost everything in life.

In Balance

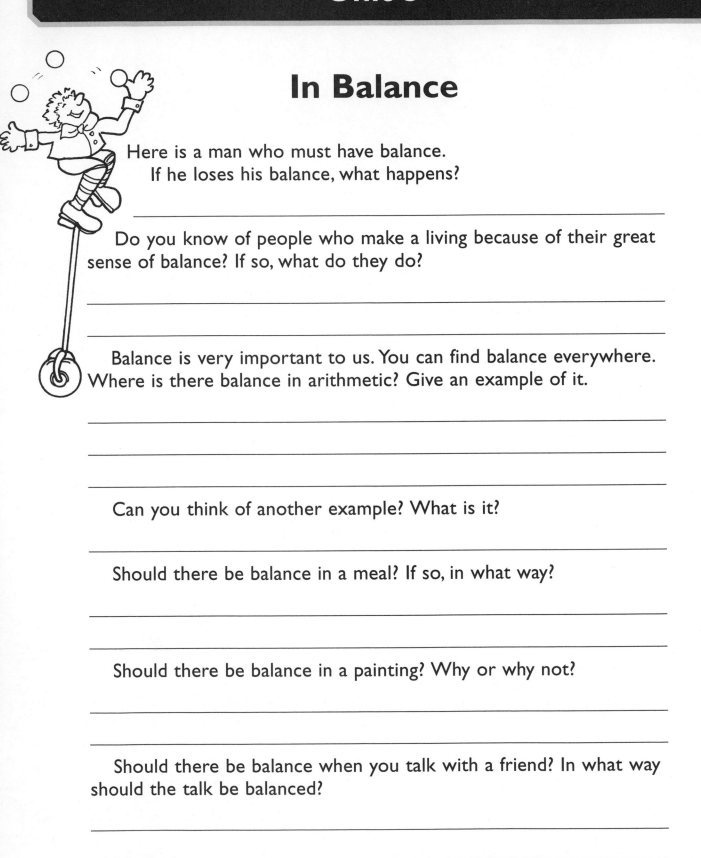

Here is a man who must have balance.
If he loses his balance, what happens?

_____

Do you know of people who make a living because of their great sense of balance? If so, what do they do?

_____

_____

Balance is very important to us. You can find balance everywhere. Where is there balance in arithmetic? Give an example of it.

_____

_____

_____

Can you think of another example? What is it?

_____

Should there be balance in a meal? If so, in what way?

_____

_____

Should there be balance in a painting? Why or why not?

_____

_____

Should there be balance when you talk with a friend? In what way should the talk be balanced?

_____

_____

What about balance on the playground? Where do you find it?

Draw a picture of it.

Tell why balance is so important in your life.

_____

_____

_____

_____

_____

AN, JU, PA, PIC, VRC ✳

Mervin's Mess

Setting the Stage for the Unit

You can administer this unit at any time, but it would be particularly appropriate during rainy weather because the problem of ants invading a dwelling is more frequent when it has been raining. Ants are great pests, but because they are so common they aren't viewed in the same way that wasps, bees, and other stinging insects are. We tend not to worry about them unless they intrude into our territory and invade our pantries. This unit is meant to put the spotlight on one aspect of their behavior. Any questions or comments about ants will serve quite well for introducing the unit.

Administering the Unit

A few of the activities that can accompany this unit are:

Developing the Naturalistic and Verbal-Linguistic Intelligences

One of the logical extensions of the simple problem posed in Mervin's Mess is to ask your students if they'd like to observe some ants and then report their findings. You can prod them with questions such as:

✳ Are the ants you see all of one size, or do you see ants of two or more sizes?
✳ Do ant trails look the same day after day, or do they change?
✳ Have you ever seen a queen ant? If not, why not?
✳ If you block ants' pathways, what happens? Do they detour around the barricade?

Developing the Visual-Spatial Intelligence

Although we instantly recognize an ant when we see it, the body parts aren't apparent at a glance. Have your students make drawings of an ant with labels for the head, thorax, abdomen, and antennae.

Developing the Interpersonal Intelligence

If enough interest in ants is generated by this unit, a team of students can be formed to investigate any of the questions missed.

Following Through

Have the children ask their parents and other adults to describe any problems they have had with ants. What do they do to get rid of them when they invade the house? Are ants unwelcome in the garden as well? This would be a good time to note that ants care for aphids in the same way that a dairy farmer cares for his cows.

An intriguing and important characteristic of ants is that they are social animals—they don't live separated from one another. You can ask the following question to provoke a good deal of thinking by your students: If you accidentally carried off a single ant when you went for a trip in a car and the ant escaped the car when you arrived at your destination, what would happen to it? Chances are that the ant would die in a short time. It would be rejected by members of another colony; and, although it might forage successfully for itself for a brief time, it must be with other ants to survive.

Mervin's Mess

Mervin stopped short as he came into the kitchen. Ants were all over the sink! His mom sure wouldn't like to see this.

"What could have brought the ants into the house?" Mervin asked himself.

Then he wondered if he should turn on the tap and try to wash them all down the drain. Since Mervin's mom was so fussy about having a very clean kitchen, he tried to see what the ants were after.

"Oh yeah," he thought. "I made a peanut butter and jelly sandwich before going to bed."

It had been raining hard for three days, and Mervin had been bored last night because he was tired of watching television. So he had a snack before going to bed.

"But I've made peanut butter and jelly sandwiches before, and the ants haven't come in. Why did they come in this time?" Mervin wondered.

What do you think caused the ants to come into Mervin's house?

_____

_____

_____

_____

_____

_____

_____

_____

There's Chew (The Chow)

Setting the Stage for the Unit

This is a simple exercise in rhyming. It isn't weighty, although you will be asking your students to think of names for pets that match each animal's nature. Otherwise, the unit is designed to give the children an opportunity to have fun with words. You can set the stage by asking your students if they have ever heard names such as Slim Jim, Tricky Dickie, Plain Jane, Handy Andy, or Ronald McDonald. These show how much people like to give nicknames that rhyme.

Administering the Unit

The following activities can be used in conjunction with There's Chew (The Chow):

Developing the Naturalistic Intelligence

Students who are keen animal lovers might want to correct classmates who choose inappropriate names for the ten pets. It will serve everyone better if they do any correcting instead of you.

Developing the Verbal-Linguistic Intelligence

This follow-up activity featuring alliteration might be given to your students if they seem to enjoy the kind of word game featured in this unit. It is like the "Hinky-Pinky" ("Hink-Pink") game but requires alliteration instead of rhyme.

What are two words with the same beginning sounds that mean:

* an unclean canine? (You can supply the first answer: dirty dog.)
* a very active honey maker? (busy bee)
* a good-looking, small horse? (pretty pony)
* an insane kitten? (crazy cat)
* an injured chicken? (hurt hen)
* an extremely dark insect? (black bug)
* an irritable young goose? (grumpy gosling)
* a bewildered young cow? (confused calf)
* a frisky young dog? (playful puppy)

Following Through

If your students particularly like one of the names in the unit, they may want to draw that animal. "Tony the Pony" or "Ms. Swish the Goldfish" might, for example, suggest a certain personality for the animal.

There's Chew (The Chow)

You might know somebody who has a pet turtle named Myrtle. Other people have pets with rhyming names—Matt the Cat, Daniel the Spaniel, and Moe the Crow. There must be at least one gorilla in a zoo named Priscilla. If you had a pet snake, what rhyming name would you give it?

_____

Maybe a better name for a puppy would be Bessie, for Messy Bessie.

Would you call your chow Chew? _____
    See if you can come up with appropriate names for these pets that rhyme. Select a name that tells something about the pet's nature.

1. pony _____

2. parrot _____

3. goldfish _____

4. pot-bellied pig _____

5. cricket _____

6. canary _____

7. rabbit _____

8. guinea pig _____

Unit 8

Holes

Setting the Stage for the Unit

There should be plenty of holes in your classroom to point to if you wish to lead into the unit with an example or two. Keyholes, gouges in desks, moth holes, vents, screens, and wastebaskets are some obvious examples. If your students have been studying earthquakes and volcanic eruptions, Holes can introduce a discussion of fissures and volcanoes that could foster the idea that students are capable of investigating these matters on their own. By thinking about analogous activities, such as digging in the sand and mining for iron ore, they can gain important insights.

Administering the Unit

Following are a few activities that can be administered in conjunction with Holes to help develop multiple intelligences:

Developing the Verbal-Linguistic Intelligence

You might have your students extend their responses about their favorite holes into a sketch or a description of their holes. Part of the unit is concerned with simple vocabulary words. This aspect of Holes can be expanded to include other words that will build your students' vocabularies: cavern, spelunker, leavened dough, running stitch, frozen dessert, and others.

Developing the Naturalistic Intelligence

In general, there are two kinds of holes: one, such as that made by the trapdoor spider, is a space that has had something constructed around it; and another, such as the knothole, is a hole that exists where something has been removed. (Do volcanoes exemplify both kinds of holes?)

Your students might surprise you by being able to see this distinction. If you present the unit to them orally, you will have an opportunity to find out. After you've gone through the questions, have the class develop a list of different kinds of holes. There should be no shortage of examples. When the list is fairly long, you and the children can reexamine the items with a view to putting them into categories. Encourage the students to think in terms of gross classifications at first. Even if they do not grasp the excavation-construction dichotomy, they will probably see other similarities and dissimilarities that may prove to be as instructive, or more so.

Developing the Visual-Spatial Intelligence

If there is time to explore the concept deeply, the children could benefit from additional activities, such as sketching different types of holes or collecting various unusual forms of apertures, interstices, and orifices. They may be able to see that some holes are in fact passages; others are really indentations; and some—there are a great many of these—are traps (that is, they open and close).

Developing the Intrapersonal Intelligence

One of the last questions of the unit asks about students' favorite holes in nature. Thoughtful students will ruminate about the question and find appropriate answers. They could come up with surprising examples of holes—the hole (opening) of a swallow's nest of mud, the mouth of a baby bird, the vortex of a whirlpool—or punch holes in binder paper, the hole in the cap of a ballpoint pen, the cavity a dentist has to fill in a tooth.

Developing the Mathematical-Logical Intelligence

You might ask your students to list and then add up the number of holes they can think of that are perfectly round, or nearly so, at their openings. A punch hole would make a good example. You can take a hole punch and demonstrate what you mean by making a hole in a piece of scratch paper. Knotholes, caves, indentations in ice cream, and holes dug in the sand are not perfectly round at the opening. Manufactured holes may or may not be perfectly round at the opening—a buttonhole is not—but they tend to be. A metal washer's hole is almost perfectly round, as is the hole in a nut for a bolt.

Following Through

If this unit does nothing else, it makes children aware of the everyday things around them. By encouraging them to be more perceptive, activities such as this can help them enjoy life more as both participants and spectators. When we use our senses more fully, we appreciate more and see possibilities for doing more. If you wish to try an informal follow-up to this unit, you might seize upon any number of simple concepts for your students to explore. For example, they could think about similar abstract notions like conjunction ("What in nature never occurs singly?") or cycles ("What repeats itself constantly?"). If you follow through with an exercise similar to Holes, allow your students to play with the idea without being pressured by time or external evaluation. Let one thing lead to another. You could see some unexpected and marvelous results.

Holes

Have you ever thought about holes? When you think of a hole, you might think of a scooped-out place in some dirt. But when Ted thinks of a hole, he thinks of a place in a fence for looking through.

His hole is called a _____ hole.

Sometimes Alice thinks of a place where a button goes when she thinks of a hole.

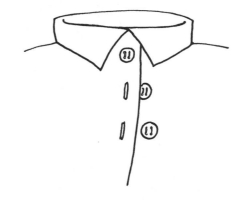

Peggy likes to dig holes in the sand.

But when she is hungry, she thinks of a hole as the middle of a small, round pastry.

Hal likes big holes. He has fun exploring caves.

What name does this hole have?

_____

Learning from Nature © 2005 • www.zephyrpress.com

Draw a picture of one of your favorite holes in nature. Under the picture, tell why you like it so much.

_____

_____

_____

_____

_____

Unit 9

Dogs

Setting the Stage for the Unit

An ideal way to lead into this unit is to read your class a humorous story about a dog. Several appropriate stories are to be found in *James Herriot's Dog Stories* (1986). The first story, about a Pekinese named Tricki-Woo, might be especially good to read. On the following day, if the children enjoy it, you might also read the third story in the book, which is also about that greedy little dog.

For children of any age, dogs constitute a favorite topic of conversation. The stage could be set for this unit almost any day. It begins in a rather routine and factual way but quickly branches out by linking dogs more intimately with people. You might find Dogs useful for introducing or augmenting a unit on pets; or you might use it as the starting point for an art lesson. However, if students answer the questions as they are presented, starting at the beginning and working through to the end, they will end up at an invitation to "write a story about a dog and its owner."

Young people often find it easier to write about animals than about human beings. They may not be any more objective about animals, but their interest in the subject will usually carry the assignment. Of course, it is not easy to write original stories about animals. Animal stories tend to direct themselves to obvious destinations by way of well-trodden paths. However, with children in the primary grades, it is not important if the story invented is trite, as long as it is real to them.

Administering the Unit

A few activities that can accompany the unit and encourage your students to learn and express themselves in preferred ways follow:

Developing the Verbal-Linguistic Intelligence

When your students have finished responding to the prompts in the unit, engage the class in a group discussion of their ideas and feelings about dogs. A good vehicle for capturing these ideas and feelings is verse. You can encourage them to offer lines for a verse in the manner of "A Boy Is . . ." and "A Girl Is . . ." A talented youngster—having been influenced, perhaps, by Charles Schulz—might get things going with a line such as "A dog is better than a warm blanket on a cold night."

Developing the Naturalistic Intelligence

Asking what your students' favorite dogs are should precipitate a lengthy discussion. They may be able to categorize dogs into groups—sporting dogs, hounds, working dogs, terriers, toy dogs, and pets. You could write the headings on the chalkboard and then list breeds for each heading as the children call them out.

Developing the Mathematical-Logical Intelligence

Breeds of dogs go in and out of fashion. Statistically minded students might welcome the challenge of finding out which dogs are most popular today. There are magazines about dogs, articles in children's periodicals, and a great deal of information about canines on the Internet for interested students to investigate.

Developing the Intrapersonal Intelligence

Your students might be inspired by the story about Tricki-Woo, or by the unit itself, and want to recount their personal experiences with dogs. They undoubtedly realize how important a pet is in their lives, but some introspection about the ways the pet affects them could be revealing.

Developing the Interpersonal Intelligence

Assign the children to groups if they seem interested in exploring a question such as "What are the most popular breeds in the United States?" (Actually, mixed-breed dogs are the most numerous, but they aren't usually sold in pet shops. You can find these dogs ready for adoption at your local animal shelter.)

Developing the Musical-Rhythmical Intelligence

If you dare to and can do so without disturbing other classes, ask your students to demonstrate how dogs differ in their barking. Do big dogs sound different than little dogs? When a dog is penned up or locked in a garage, does it bark differently from the way it barks when another dog comes by? What are the differences in rhythm?

Following Through

It is quite possible that, after they have completed this unit, students may look at people inside and outside of the classroom differently. It's an age-old reaction, once the suggestion has been given, to see humans in dogs' faces and dogs' faces in humans. Since much has been made of the ways in which dogs can be made to resemble humans by giving them one or two articles of apparel (you might show your class one of the famous paintings of dogs playing cards) and of people's tendency to select as pets dogs that resemble themselves, you will probably feel that there is no need to emphasize the "dogginess" of man. On the other hand, you may want to explore the resemblance between other kinds of animals and humans. Cats, horses, fish (especially those the children know as household pets or as the focal points of fishing expeditions), and birds might be excellent animals to discuss and to compare with people.

Paul Gallico's *The Silent Miaow* (1964) should give almost any class ideas for stories written from the point of view of pets speaking to other pets. *The Silent Miaow* is described as "a manual for kittens, strays, and homeless cats translated from cat language and edited by Paul Gallico." It gives advice to other cats about how to win friends and influence people and describes many of the cat's exploits. Children who have pets could be asked to act as "ghost writers" or "translators" for their own pets, telling about life from the pet's point of view and giving advice to other pets about people. Young children would enjoy bringing photographs of their pets and describing their adventures.

Unit 9

Dogs

This is a well-known kind of dog. What kind of dog is it?

_____

How did this dog get its name?

_____

What do you like about this dog?

_____

What can it do well?

_____

It is said that some dogs look like their owners.
Does this dog look like any person you know? Who?

_____

Why does it look like this person?

_____

_____

Does this dog act like anyone you know? Who?

_____

How are the actions of the dog like that person's?

_____

_____

This is another popular breed of dog. What kind of dog is it?

_____

Learning from Nature © 2005 • www.zephyrpress.com

Can you guess how this breed got its name?

_____

What word best describes one of these dogs?

_____

Can you think of any people you know with this trait? Who?

_____

What does a sheepdog do well?

_____

Does this kind of dog act like anyone you know? Who?

_____

How do the person and the sheepdog act the same?

_____

Write a story about a dog and its owner in the space below.

_____

_____

_____

_____

_____

_____

_____

Unit 10

Animal Talk

Setting the Stage for the Unit

People try to make the voices of animals conform to human speech, and in some cases our words and the animal sounds are fairly close. In this unit your students are asked to come up with six words that are commonly associated with the sounds the animals often make. None of the items should stump your students. You might begin the unit by looking with the children at the illustration of the horse "naying" at a town meeting. We usually spell the horse's sound as "neighing," but it is unclear why we do.

Administering the Unit

The first six questions are answered by (1) Who, (2) Quack, (3) Bah, (4) Peep, (5) Rough, and (6) Cheap. The unit becomes more challenging when your students get to the last two prompts. Some of them might think of these additional animal "words": honk, fit (the "phtt!" of a cat enraged), croak, hiss, bark (a seal makes this sound quite well), or coo. Of course, several birds are very good at mimicking human speech. Although any number of responses to the last prompt are possible, one of the obvious ones is that the owl could say, "Who?", and the duck could reply with "Quack," and the sheep could respond, in turn, with "Bah!"

The following are two of the activities that can accompany the unit:

Developing the Naturalistic and Verbal-Linguistic Intelligences

You might have your students listen for animal sounds for a day or two after finishing this unit, or you can administer it just before a field trip to a zoo or farm. The students can report what they have heard, and then they can attempt to transcribe the sounds into written words—or at least letters that represent the sounds that they heard.

Developing the Mathematical-Logical Intelligence

You and the children can count the number of sounds heard and also record their frequencies. Before doing so, you might ask the children to guess which sounds will probably be the ones most often heard by the class.

Following Through

The idea of animals talking to one another is trite, of course, but you might ask your students to think of some dialogue between these unlikely pairs of animals:

* a salamander and a catfish
* a dog and a squirrel
* a bee and a grasshopper
* a cat and a cow
* a mosquito and a spider
* a horse and a goat
* a seal and a dolphin

As most of your students know, in E. B. White's *Charlotte's Web* there is charming and inspiring dialogue between a spider and a pig. The children can create the dialogue together in a group activity, or they can make up their imaginary dialogue in dyads or by themselves.

Animal Talk

Animals make sounds that sound like words sometimes. For instance, what sound does a horse make that is meant to be a "no" vote at a meeting? _____

What sound does an owl make that is like someone asking a question?

_____

What sound does a duck make that is like a word that means "bad doctor"? _____

What sound does a sheep make that is like someone doubting a person's word? _____

What sound does a baby bird make that also describes someone taking a quick look at something? _____

What sound does a dog make that is the answer to this question:

What is the opposite of smooth?

_____

What sound does a chick make that sounds like the word for a bargain?

_____

What other sounds do animals make that seem like words?

_____

Could an animal make a sound that seems to respond to another animal's sound? What animals could do that?

_____

Unit 11

Funny Bunnies

Setting the Stage for the Unit

If the class has recently read a story about rabbits or hares, you could use that as a lead-in to this unit. If you administer it in a month such as April or May, the unit will be topical. You can ask, "What, if anything, does the bunny have to defend itself?" Actually, those hind feet can deliver a good kick.

The central concept is that animals have various ways of defending themselves. We aren't serious about crossing a porcupine and a bunny. However, bunnies, or rabbits, are regarded by carnivorous animals as prey and could use the porcupine's quills or the skunk's musk pouch to fend off their enemies.

Administering the Unit

A few of the activities that can accompany the administration of Funny Bunnies are:

Developing the Naturalistic and Verbal-Linguistic Intelligences

Possibly one, or more, of your students keeps rabbits and would be willing to share with the class all the work that this entails. As with other pets, rabbits require food, water, and a clean place in which to live. To teach their children responsibility, parents let them get dogs, cats, rabbits, hamsters, horses, canaries, goldfish, and more. However, the parents often end up doing most, if not all, of the work necessary for keeping the pets alive and healthy. The child in your class who is conscientious about raising one or more rabbits could be the exception to the above

generalization. If so, he or she can explain how important water, diet, and sanitation are to a pet.

Developing the Mathematical-Logical Intelligence

Take a census of the pets your students presently have. The children can name the kinds of pets and their number ("I have one dog and two cats and a goldfish"), and the total number can be added up as well as the total number of animal species. The children should also be able to tell approximately how long they have had each of their pets. Since they won't be required to calculate percentages as part of the arithmetic curriculum, they can simply look at the tallies for each kind of pet and note the most popular. Before they do, you might ask them to predict which pet will be the most popular among their classmates.

Following Through

Your students might not know much more about rabbits than the mythical Easter Bunny and the cartoon character Bugs Bunny. If that is so, they should learn more about these interesting animals. You can encourage them to consult books or people who raise rabbits for the answers to the following questions:

* Why isn't a jackrabbit a rabbit?
* Do all rabbits have pink eyes?
* Why do rabbits have such long ears?
* What rabbits are raised for their fur?
* Where does the snowshoe rabbit live?
* How do rabbits fight one another?

Unit 11

Funny Bunnies

Over a long period of time, animals change. These changes can help their species from dying out. Many animals have changed in ways to keep other animals from eating them.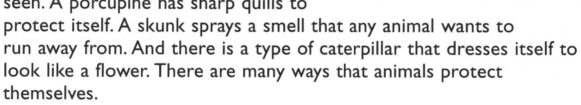

Some butterflies have bright colors, warning birds not to eat them. An octopus squirts out a cloud of ink so it can't be seen. A porcupine has sharp quills to protect itself. A skunk sprays a smell that any animal wants to run away from. And there is a type of caterpillar that dresses itself to look like a flower. There are many ways that animals protect themselves.

Except for being able to run fast, a bunny can't defend itself too well. What if bunnies had quills to defend themselves? What could happen?

_____

_____

_____

Or what if a bunny could do what a skunk can do? What could happen then?

_____

_____

_____

_____

Unit 12

Which Doesn't Fit?

Setting the Stage for the Unit

The theme of this unit is things belonging in their proper context. You might demonstrate by showing your students a bowl of fruit with a pair of pliers sticking out from the middle. "What is out of place?" you can ask. They will readily see that the pliers do not belong with the apple, orange, pear, banana, or whatever else you have in the bowl.

Administering the Unit

Following are some ways that Which Doesn't Fit? can be used to help develop your students' multiple intelligences:

Developing the Visual-Spatial Intelligence

Your students' first task in this unit is to draw a thing that can be substituted for the one that is out of place in the illustration (the basketball-tossing baseball player). Their second task is to draw three or four people, one of whom doesn't fit with the others. Aside from the challenge of thinking of appropriate subjects, the students face the challenge of drawing them so that they are recognizable. The children who love to draw will enjoy this test of their skills.

Developing the Mathematical-Logical Intelligence

Ask your students about the situations in which the athletes appear in the third illustration, although the baseball player is performing in a most unusual way.

You could also ask what the athletes have in common.

Developing Interpersonal Intelligence

Since the final task is to draw four people, one of whom doesn't fit with the others, the students who have good social skills, or who are aware of how people with a lot in common tend to associate with each other, will produce drawings that will graphically exhibit the similarities and the one glaring difference.

Following Through

The basic idea of Which Doesn't Fit? can be used to introduce ideas in math ("Which doesn't fit—1, 3, 5, 6, or 7?"), social studies (place a palm tree in a setting with a polar bear and an igloo), or home economics (display a pair of scissors, a knife, and tongs).

You can also take the best of your students' efforts to portray the four people (one of whom doesn't fit) and give it to the class as a follow-up exercise. There is a lot to be said for this idea. The students whose drawings are selected are rewarded, and the children themselves will be thinking at their own level about things that interest them. Being careful not to make too much of it, you can have the child whose drawing is presented to the class create another puzzle while the rest of the class is working on theirs.

Which Doesn't Fit?

Which one should be someplace else? Circle it.

Now look at the thing you circled. What can you put in its place? On a separate piece of paper draw the thing that does fit, then cut it out and paste it over the thing that doesn't fit.

Now, draw a picture of three or four people. Draw one that doesn't fit with the others.

Why doesn't one of the people in your drawing fit?

_____

_____

Unit 13

Quakes

Setting the Stage for the Unit

There are many earthquakes occurring somewhere on our planet every hour of every day. It is estimated that there may be as many as a million earthquakes each year. Very often people in the affected areas don't even notice these tremors. When the quakes are strong enough, though, a great many people can be hurt or killed, and property damage can be extensive. If your school is located in a zone that has a fault, the building undoubtedly has been tested and shown to be safe in the event of an earthquake. To warm up your students for this unit, ask them if they have heard of an earthquake anywhere recently.

Administering the Unit

A few of the activities that might accompany this unit are:

Developing the Naturalistic Intelligence

Ask your students if they know how the size of an earthquake is measured. A few may be able to mention the Richter scale because nearly every report about an earthquake given on a television or radio newscast will report its strength in terms of a reading on the Richter scale. Each number on the Richter scale represents an earthquake ten times as strong as one of the next lower magnitude. If an earthquake is measured at seven in Japan, it will be ten times as strong as a six. Ask your students which animals would most likely be disturbed by a mild earthquake. Those children who are intrigued by earthquakes and volcanoes can obtain more information about them in periodicals and books, and on the Internet. The Saturday edition of our newspaper presents a weekly summary of seismic activity in the area.

Developing the Intrapersonal Intelligence

The prompts in Quakes are meant to elicit the feelings the children would have if an earthquake were to strike their community. It's very hard for adults to know what their reactions and emotions might be if they were in an earthquake, so we don't suppose young children will be eloquent about imagining such an experience. Nevertheless, because earthquakes are as prevalent as they are—even in states where they are quite unusual, they can occur—it is a good idea for children to be intellectually and emotionally prepared for such an event.

Developing the Verbal-Linguistic Intelligence

You can have your students write a story about the rescue of a person or an animal during or after an earthquake.

Following Through

One school district has issued these instructions to its students if an earthquake occurs:
All children/students, K–12, are taught as follows:

DUCK . . . (or DROP)

COVER . . .

HOLD . . .

When a teacher says "Duck, Cover, and Hold," all students in any classroom in the state must stop whatever they are doing and comply at once. Students must also: (1) turn away from windows, (2) crouch under a desk or table, (3) put both hands on the back of their necks and tuck their heads down, and (4) hold onto the desk or table. The state mandates that the students must practice this drill at least four times a year. Compare these instructions to the ones that are given in your district.

Quakes

Every now and then the earth shakes a lot. When it shakes so that the ground moves and pictures fall off walls, we say there has been an earthquake. *Quake* means to shake or tremble. After reading reports of large earthquakes in the news, many people get scared when the ground moves. Most earthquakes are small and don't do much damage, but very strong earthquakes can make buildings fall and people can get hurt.

People can also get hurt in big storms and in fires. When a storm approaches, reports from ships at sea and airplanes in the sky warn us. As yet, we don't have good ways of telling when an earthquake is coming.

It is not likely that you will ever be hurt in an earthquake, but you should know that people do get hurt in earthquakes. People must think about what damage earthquakes do and protect themselves if one happens. What does your teacher say you must do in an earthquake?

_____

_____

_____

How would you feel if you rescued a cat or dog in an earthquake?

_____

_____

How would you feel if someone took you by the hand and led you to safety in an earthquake? _____

_____

How would you feel if you saw someone running and yelling in an earthquake? _____

_____

Unit 14

To Catch a Frog

Setting the Stage for the Unit

When they are young, children naturally like to catch things, especially small animals. To lead into the unit you might bring a sample of your own collecting, if you have one or more collections, and then ask if anyone has caught any small creatures recently. Perhaps one child has even caught a frog.

Administering the Unit

A few of the activities that could accompany To Catch a Frog are:

Developing the Naturalistic Intelligence

The prompts in this unit should trigger a discussion of what qualifies as good collecting. There are, after all, many plants, animals, and minerals that should not be taken from their places in nature. Wildflowers, for example, shouldn't be picked, and many of your students have probably learned that wildflowers soon lose their beauty and appeal if they are picked. One young boy brought home several baby trout that he had scooped out of a creek. After his uncle convinced him that the trout could grow better in the creek than in a fish bowl, the boy returned them to the wild. Should children catch frogs? What happens when they take the frogs home?

Developing the Visual-Spatial Intelligence

Invite children who have collections to show them and talk about them. The collection can be inanimate, such as arrowheads, seashells, and rocks, or animate, such as tropical fish and parakeets.

Developing the Visual-Spatial and Interpersonal Intelligences

If the students show enough interest in collections, they could collaborate by collecting insects, rocks, leaves, and more, and then mounting them in a display.

Following Through

This unit raises the question of what kind of weather is best for frog catching. It could devolve into a discussion of the best weather for catching fish. People who fish are utterly convinced that the weather and the time of day affect fishing. Is there scientific evidence that supports their belief?

Unit 14

To Catch a Frog

Let's imagine you are going outside today. You want to catch a frog. You think it is a good day to catch a frog. If it is a good day to catch a frog . . .
   Is it hot or cold, or in between?

_____

   What does the sky look like?

_____

   Is the sun shining?

_____

   If not, is there rain or fog or snow?

_____

   Draw a picture below of where you will catch the frog. How will you show what the weather will be like?

_____

O, PIC, S, VRC ✳

Unit 15

Water

Setting the Stage for the Unit

With the possible exception of air, water is the most precious element on earth. Living things can't do without it. You might point this fact out and also that the availability and the purity of water have become two of humankind's greatest problems in the twenty-first century.

Administering the Unit

Among the activities that can accompany this unit are the following:

Developing the Naturalistic Intelligence

Children who are outdoors a good deal are likely to respond fluently to the questions in Water, but those who have read widely are also likely to contribute a great deal. Those who have had experiences near or on the ocean can be expected to produce sound ideas about how the ocean will help people in the future. One or two may have even heard of desalinization (removing the salt from water) efforts being conducted on our nation's coasts.

Developing the Verbal-Linguistic Intelligence

In addition to contributing their ideas about water's role in the future, your students might want to learn more about the subject by exploring what is presented on the Internet. All of the conservation organizations, including the Sierra Club, Audubon Society, National Wildlife Federation, Nature Conservancy, and Friends of the Earth, have Web sites and offer current information about the water conservation problems that are plaguing us.

Developing the Musical-Rhythmical Intelligence

Some of the facts that your students learn can be expressed in jingles, songs, and slogans.

Following Through

Whereas once we thought of the oceans as boundless sources of life—and vast dumping receptacles—we now realize that many ecosystems in the seas are fragile and are being terribly damaged. Your students should be encouraged to look seriously at this growing problem. They aren't too young to learn about the degradations that are happening in the world.

Water

Because water covers most of the world, people have always thought about it. Sometimes we think of water because our animals or plants need it. Other times we think of it because it comes down from the sky and gets us wet. Most of the things in the world that are alive are in water.

Write down one thing we can do with water.

_____

What are some of the other things we might do with water?

_____

_____

What can we find in an ocean?

_____

More and more people are thinking of the ocean when they think of how many hungry people there are in the world. Why is that?

_____

_____

In the years ahead people will try to use the oceans to help people. How do you think oceans can be used to help people?

_____

_____

Some day we might have undersea colonies where people will live and work. What do you think such an underwater city or colony would look like? Draw a picture of how you think it would look.

At the Bottom of the Sea

Setting the Stage for the Unit

This unit is meant to sharpen your students' ability to get information by questioning. To lead into the unit you might ask your students how they get most of their information. When they are young, before they can read, youngsters are full of questions about things they want to know about. "Why?" is a much-used word by children. At the second- or third-grade level, questions may not be as important to them as observing, listening, or reading are. It would be interesting to learn how they respond to such a question as "How do you get most of your information?" Would you expect them to answer "Television"?

Administering the Unit

A few of the activities that might accompany At the Bottom of the Sea are:

Developing the Naturalistic and Mathematical-Logical Intelligences

The topic of underwater colonization is addressed in the unit. It is probable that your students haven't encountered the concept as yet. They may have some knowledge of experiments in living in space, because those have been taking place for some time now. Living at the bottom of the sea, though, will probably be a new concept to them, and it could very well excite their imaginations. As in space, there are certain important restrictions and constraints when humans try to live beneath the surface of the ocean. Ask your students what these are. They will know that breathing air is one of the first considerations. Have them think about what the others might be.

Developing the Intrapersonal Intelligence

Just as people respond in a variety of ways to the idea that we could live permanently in space, they have diverse reactions to the proposal that we establish undersea colonies. Ask your students what their reaction would be if they found out they were going to live in an undersea colony.

Developing the Visual-Spatial Intelligence

The illustration at the bottom of the page is meant to be humorous and is not meant to give your students an idea of an undersea living situation. Without their doing any research about the matter of establishing an undersea colony, have your students draw their ideas about what such an underwater dwelling would be like. Some of them might have seen a film version of Jules Verne's *20,000 Leagues under the Sea*. If so, some of the ideas in the film can be shared.

Following Through

Your students can check their ideas about an undersea colony by looking into reference books and periodicals. The bathyscaph and other underwater vehicles have been successfully operating on the ocean floor for many years. Your students should be able to obtain information about the structure of the more advanced vehicles doing oceanographic research. They can try to find out how long people have been able to stay in them.

Let's imagine that you have won a big prize. Your name was picked from a large number of names in a contest. You get to have dinner with a famous scientist. She has lived for six months on the bottom of the sea. The scientist has been studying all of the creatures and plant life that live there. You are very interested in talking with her because you have heard that she saw things that no one has seen before. She has also lived in the sea longer than anyone else has.

   What will you ask her? Think of at least six questions to ask the scientist.

_____

_____

_____

_____

_____

_____

_____

_____

Unit 17

Fished Out

Setting the Stage for the Unit

Fisheries (that part of the ocean where fishermen fish) on all of our coasts are being depleted or wiped out. This has caused an upheaval in the lives of people who rely on the fishing industry for a living. If you live near an ocean, river, lake, or bay that has had its stock of fishes depleted, lead into this unit with a comment or two about what has happened and is happening to our fisheries. If you are not located near one of these areas, you might ask your students if fish is regularly on the menu at home and if it is always the same kind of fish.

Administering the Unit

A few of the activities that can accompany the unit are:

Developing the Naturalistic Intelligence

Ask your students if they know how the pollution of rivers and creeks can affect fish. You can describe what happens when a river is polluted: untreated sewage and industrial chemicals add nutrients, poisons, heat, and solid material to a river. This reduces the oxygen content by increasing algae and bacteria in the water. As a result, fish and freshwater invertebrates disappear. Also, when an alien species of fish is introduced to a river or lake, it can reduce or eliminate many native fish. Brown trout, for instance, have been introduced as game fish in lakes and rivers and have depopulated them of other species.

Developing the Verbal-Linguistic Intelligence

This unit should encourage your students to learn more about the problems of disappearing fisheries; pollution of oceans, lakes, and rivers; and the shifting economy. All of these are very big topics, but your students can inform themselves by consulting material at their reading level in books, in periodicals, and on the Internet.

The children should not attempt to respond to the final questions of the unit without first doing some research about the problem. Interviewing people in the fishing industry would be advisable if you are located close to places where people are employed fishing or processing fish.

Following Through

If you are fortunate enough to have a person in your community who makes a living by fishing or processing fish, it is a good bet that he or she would jump at the chance to talk to your class about the problems people in the fishing industry are facing.

Unit 17

Fished Out

Mona's father is a fisherman. He has been a fisherman since before Mona was born. For the past three years Mona's father hasn't caught many fish. There have been very few fish in the sea to catch.

After the poor catch last season, Mona's mother asked her husband to find another job. He said, "Fishing is the only thing I know how to do." So he fished this season, and the catch was even worse.

Mona doesn't want to move to another town, but all of the fishermen in her town are becoming very poor. They say that the fishing is going to be poor next year, too. If they moved, Mona would miss her friends in the third grade, but she knows her mother is right. Her father should find another job.

What suggestion do you have for Mona and her family?

_____

_____

If there is a poor catch again next year, they will not be able to afford their house payments. What should they do?

_____

_____

_____

_____

_____

_____

AN, BT, JU, PA, S ✺

Unit 18

Catching a Water Beetle

Setting the Stage for the Unit

This is another problem-solving unit. It's about a boy and the difficulties he encounters while trying to catch a water beetle. Assuming that many of your students have tried to catch insects or other small creatures, they should have some interest in finding out how Fred is able to catch his beetle. To set the stage for the unit, you could bring to class a small creature from a pond and describe to your class how you captured it. Some pond residents are found nearly everywhere, and you should be able to catch anything from a pollywog to a mosquito larva (the one we could never catch was the strider).

Administering the Unit

A few of the ways that Catching a Water Beetle can be used to encourage your students to develop their multiple intelligences are as follows:

Developing the Naturalistic Intelligence

Although some children aren't attracted to an activity such as catching a bug, there will be those in your class who are already collectors of butterflies and moths and who spend considerable amounts of time observing ants, caterpillars, snails, and even earthworms. They will enjoy thinking about Fred's excursion to the pond.

Developing the Mathematical-Logical Intelligence

Having some experience in catching little creatures in ponds and streams would help a child solve Fred's problem, but your students should be able to come up with a logical solution just by using reason. For one thing, it is clear that certain kinds of containers won't do the job. The child who has done a good deal of fishing might think of a net with mesh fine enough to contain the water beetle.

Developing the Visual-Spatial Intelligence

Some children may be able to show how they would catch the water beetle by diagramming or drawing their solution. If so, they should be encouraged to do so.

Developing the Verbal-Linguistic Intelligence

Your students will find it challenging to describe in written words how they would catch the elusive water beetle. They will need to use a few words that they haven't written before, and spelling those words correctly could seem daunting. Assist them if you must, but encourage them to use dictionaries, reference books, and perhaps the Internet when they try to describe their solutions.

Following Through

You might follow through with this unit by opening up some of the ecological aspects of collecting creatures from ponds, streams, lakes, or the countryside. For example, you might say something like this:

> A boy I know used to go to a nearby creek and catch baby trout. One time, he brought the baby trout home in a jar and then put them in a fishbowl. They seemed to survive for a while in the fishbowl, but when he went back to the creek to catch some more baby trout for the fishbowl his parents objected. Why didn't they want him to bring more baby trout home? What eventually would happen to baby trout in a fishbowl?

Catching a Water Beetle

Fred was stumped. He didn't know what to do.
His teacher had asked him to catch a water
beetle. She knew there was a pond near where
Fred lived. So she asked him to find a water
beetle in the pond. Fred was unhappy because
each time he tried to scoop up a water
beetle, it got away.

Water beetles can breathe
underwater because they catch air
underneath their bodies. They use
that air for breathing when they are
under the water. They have flat legs
for swimming.

Water beetles are also quick—quicker
than Fred. He kept trying to catch a water beetle in a jar. He couldn't
catch one. Then he tried a larger jar. Still no luck. Finally, Fred used a
two-gallon bucket. That didn't work either.

Fred was about to give up when he had an idea. "That might
work," Fred said out loud.

What was Fred's idea?

_____

_____

_____

_____

_____

_____

Unit 19

Nan Meets a Bird

Setting the Stage for the Unit

A person can live for many years near birds, mammals, and reptiles and have no idea about their names or habits. Not so for Nan. She is an observant seven-year-old who already understands the ways of a red-winged blackbird. Ask your students if they have ever seen a bird with black feathers and red epaulets. If one or more have, ask them to describe what they saw to the class. The rest of the unit, however, should be tackled individually. Have a class discussion when your students have finished drawing a picture of Nan and the bird.

Administering the Unit

A few of the activities that work well with Nan Meets a Bird are:

Developing the Naturalistic Intelligence

The students who know about birds that dive-bomb during mating season will probably also know the names of birds that harass people who come too close to their nests. It would be a good idea for you to challenge your students, however, and ask them to learn the names of at least three other birds that aggressively patrol the area near their nests.

Developing the Verbal-Linguistic Intelligence

Have your students write more about Nan and her experiences on her walks. Discuss words that convey the idea of blackbirds in flight ("swooping," "diving," "darting," "dive-bombing," and the like). Help your students develop vocabularies that allow them to express adequately the movements, moods, reactions, and settings that should be present in their stories about Nan.

Developing the Bodily-Kinesthetic Intelligence

Some students might be willing to pantomime the action in the story, or in the story that they write about Nan and her adventures.

Following Through

One or more of the children's stories can be turned into a skit and performed for the class. The authors of these chosen stories can be made directors, and they can rehearse their little companies.

Unit 19

Nan Meets a Bird

Nan loved to walk. When she was three, she always skipped and ran. But now that she had turned seven, she mostly walked. On this day, she walked because the rain had stopped. The sunshine made everything sparkle. Nan also wanted to get a book from the library.

Just before she reached the library, Nan looked up into a big tree. She saw a bird in the tree. It was all black except for bright red patches on its wings.

The bird did not move at first. It looked at Nan. Then, as Nan walked on, the bird flew right at her. Nan ducked her head, and the bird swooshed over her. The bird surprised Nan, but she wasn't scared. She knew that the bird had dived at her for a good reason.

Why do you think the bird flew right at Nan?

_____

_____

Could there be another reason?

_____

_____

Can you think of a better title for this story? What is it?

_____

Draw a picture of Nan and the bird on the back of this sheet.

Unit 20

Just Like a Crow

Setting the Stage for the Unit

Some people are fond of crows, but they are in the minority. One or more of your students could say yes if you ask whether any of them like crows, but most won't, principally because of the raucous bird's noisy ways. Crows are known to be thieves and will steal any glittering object that they spy.

Administering the Unit

A few of the activities that can be used with Just Like a Crow are:

Developing the Naturalistic Intelligence

The series of questions posed in Just Like a Crow will be easy enough to answer for the children who like to watch birds. Invariably, crows are aggressive toward other birds. They only seem to be intimidated by owls, and a flock of crows will even harass an owl. Crows carry sticks around in their mouths to build their rough nests, but they carry a great variety of food and other objects as well.

Developing the Verbal-Linguistic Intelligence

If the children are interested in crows, it shouldn't be hard to get them to relate their experiences with the corvids. Crows are apparently ubiquitous—you find them everywhere, even though they have been bombed and poisoned as much or more than any bird.

Following Through

The following are questions that you can ask to get the children thinking about crows and wanting to know more about them:

Crows

Crows are intelligent and have excellent eyesight. They are strong fliers and are quick to perceive danger. You don't see dead crows on the highway. They are not choosy about what they eat. They will eat young birds, baby mice, eggs, insects, reptiles, grain, fruits, and carrion. Their bills can be used to hammer, crack, crush, probe, split, and tear. They may gather in flocks by the thousands. Scouts from a flock will often precede it into a new feeding territory. When danger threatens a flock that's feeding, sentinels sound the alarm. Crows lay from four to six eggs, which are greenish with brown spots. Both male and female brood; the incubation period lasts up to 18 days. In about five weeks the fledglings leave the nest.

* What are the differences between a crow and a raven?
* Why do some bird lovers dislike crows?
* Why have forest loggers and hunters hurt some kinds of birds more than they have crows, whose numbers continue to increase?
* Why do you sometimes see three or four blackbirds chasing and circling a crow?

Just Like a Crow

Jay lived in the city, but he had four big trees in his backyard. One sunny day, Jay and his mother were having lunch in the backyard. Jay's mother looked up and saw a crow in one of the trees.

"It may be a young one," Jay's mother said, "because its mouth is open. Maybe it wants to be fed."

Jay was fond of most birds, but he did not like crows. He looked up at the bird, and its mouth was still open. No other crow was in that tree.

"I don't think it's a baby because it's too big," said Jay.

"Well, they get big fast," said his mother.

Ten minutes later, Jay looked up into the tree and saw the same crow.

"I think it has something in its mouth," Jay told his mother. "It still has its mouth open."

Jay was right. The crow had something in its mouth. Crows like to steal things. Other birds don't like crows. Why don't other birds like them?

_____

_____

What kinds of things do crows carry around in their mouths?

_____

_____

What do you think was inside this crow's mouth? Why?

_____

_____

_____

_____

_____

Unit 21

Sing Like the Birds

Setting the Stage for the Unit

If you plan to administer this unit at a time when birds are singing regularly in the morning, as they do in spring, you can call attention to their cheerful songs. The mockingbird's repertory is enough to give your students a rundown of these songs, if you are lucky enough to have mockers in the area. Not every child pays a great deal of attention to the sounds of birds, so it is important to expose your students to some prominent bird songs and calls. There are excellent recordings of bird songs and calls, and you may wish to play some on a tape recorder or CD player. (National Geographic's *Bird Songs of Garden, Woodland, and Meadow* is recommended.)

Administering the Unit

Some activities that can be used with Sing Like the Birds and will encourage your students to develop their multiple intelligences follow:

Developing the Naturalistic Intelligence

Along with knowing the calls and songs of birds, the child who volunteers to do the imitating will probably be able to provide a good deal of additional information about the nests, territories, feeding habits, enemies, and plumage of birds. If so, this may be the most important outcome of the unit. A few of the birds that get their common names from the sounds they make are the whip-poor-will, the chickadee, the phoebe, and the bobwhite.

Developing the Musical-Rhythmical Intelligence

The unit ends with an invitation for the students to imitate birdcalls and songs. In some regions of the country (many rural areas, for example), a young, expert birdcall imitator could go on for an hour or more. In most other areas, however, a teacher would be lucky to have one student who could imitate a single bird song or call. Youngsters who have mastered a birdcall or two are usually willing to demonstrate their talent.

Developing the Visual-Spatial Intelligence

The bird that illustrates the unit can be colored, and your students can also draw or trace the outline of other birds and color them. The United States has had several great illustrators of birds, such as John James Audubon and Ralph Tory Peterson. If at all possible, you should show your students some of their work.

Following Through

If the children become quite interested in songbirds, they can make drawings of the most common ones and display them in the room. The mockingbird, robin, thrush, thrasher, meadowlark, bluebird, cardinal, and wren are favorite songbirds. Of course, the ones that are common in your area are the birds that your students will want to depict and display.

Sing Like the Birds

Most birds sing because they want to let other birds know they "own" the space where they are. It is their territory. The males also sing to attract the females.

Does a caged bird sing because it is happy?

_____

Why or why not?

_____

_____

Many birds get their names from the sounds of their songs or calls. Can you think of one? What is it?

_____

Name three songbirds that live near you.

_____

_____

_____

Some boys and girls can imitate bird songs and calls. Can you?

_____

Name three animals that would be easier to find if they sang.

_____

_____

_____

_____

A January Mystery

Setting the Stage for the Unit

A number of occasions might be opportune for administering this lesson: a cold day in January; the day your class makes a feeding tray for birds, or the day your class discusses the project; a day when you and your students feel the need to give some variety to the reading program; or a day when you would like to provide some practice in making hypotheses and testing them. The students also practice adding and subtracting when they attempt to solve the mystery, so you may find the unit helpful in reinforcing those arithmetic skills. Fundamentally, it is a reading lesson, however. Most primary children will have to read the story carefully before they can start to solve the mystery.

Administering the Unit

Following are some ideas about how A January Mystery can be administered and how students with preferred ways of learning can be encouraged to develop their talents:

Developing the Naturalistic Intelligence

Some of your students might be keen observers of birds, and they could know quite a bit about jays. Jays and their cousins the crows are thieves, and one or more children could mention this fact. Whether that characteristic would figure into a solution to the mystery is a tantalizing question.

Developing the Verbal-Linguistic Intelligence

Although you may prefer to read the story to your students, it is a good plan to have them read it silently. As you would for any reading lesson, you can

go over any words that might cause some of your students difficulty and, afterward, you can ask a few questions about the story to test their comprehension of its contents.

As is the case with many of the units in this book, A January Mystery can be attacked logically or imaginatively. For example, one child might hypothesize that *someone else* has been feeding those birds also. Another might suppose that the King of the Jays had ordered his subjects to return an equal amount of corn to the tray after the first day, because he wanted to share the food with other birds. (In real life jays are bullies and not inclined to share with other species.) The jay that was delegated to do the job got mixed up and put four kernels back and then, realizing his mistake, five more on the following day.

Developing the Mathematical-Logical Intelligence

After you are satisfied that your students understand the main points of the story, set them to work hypothesizing about how more kernels of corn ended up on the feeding tray than had been placed there originally. Give them enough time to think through the problem and to generate several hypotheses. Several of your students will be able to come up with a solution almost immediately, and they may be "dying" to tell their classmates. But hold them off until the others have had a chance to think about the mystery. The children can share their ideas when everyone has had a chance to do some thinking.

Developing the Bodily-Kinesthetic Intelligence

If a student has worked out a solution to the mystery, he or she might want to explain it by acting out what happened with the jays and the kernels of corn. The demonstration will make the student's solution clear.

Developing the Visual-Spatial Intelligence

Although many of your students won't have the artistic skills to do so, one or more might be able to draw a picture of the scene of the noisy jays and the feeding tray. There may be a "birder" in your class who can give information about the jay's physical characteristics, whether the local species is blue, scrub, green, Steller's, gray, or another kind.

Following Through

A January Mystery might make your students interested in birds and their ways. The jay is among the most colorful of birds—both physically and behaviorally—and your students may want to find out more about them. Jays are found everywhere because they have adapted very well to the areas where humans live. Crows are also fascinating (and often obnoxious). Your students may want to learn about them and other corvids such as the magpie. They are all great mimics.

A January Mystery

One cold day in January, the children in Mrs. Carter's class saw several jays near the school yard. Since the ground was covered with snow, the children were worried that the birds wouldn't have enough to eat. They decided to leave some food on a feeding tray for the jays so the birds would not starve.

The next day the children left some suet, bread crumbs, and seven kernels of corn. When they looked at the tray on the following day, the bread crumbs and suet were gone, but there were four kernels of corn left. The children put more bread crumbs and suet on the tray. They didn't put any more corn on the tray. When they looked at the tray on the third day, the suet and breadcrumbs were gone again—but there were nine kernels of corn on the tray!

Can you explain why there were nine kernels of corn on the tray? What might have happened?

_____

_____

_____

_____

_____

_____

_____

_____

_____

Learning from Nature © 2005 • www.zephyrpress.com

A Lot of Air

Setting the Stage for the Unit

Two elements that are more or less free on this planet are air and water. In urban situations water is rarely free, but in many parts of the world it is. Except for some gasoline stations that sell air for the tires of cars, air is free—if sometimes polluted—everywhere. You could lead in to this unit by asking your students: "What is all around us, is free, and we can't live without it?"

Administering the Unit

The following are a few suggestions for activities that you might use to encourage the development of multiple intelligences in your students:

Developing the Naturalistic Intelligence

Perhaps there are students in your class who have given considerable thought to air. The subject is much more in the news now than it was 50 years ago, before the spread of air pollution throughout the country. At that time there were a few places, such as Pittsburgh (which has subsequently cleaned up its atmosphere) where the air quality was famously poor. Now newspapers almost everywhere in the country record the air-quality readings. Most of your students will be well aware of air pollution, but some of them may have given a little more thought than others to the role air plays in their lives (air for balloons, breathing, bubbles, bicycle tires, beach balls, basketball balls, etc.). The oceans are the engines that create air currents. The differences in temperature between masses of air are responsible for air movement.

Developing the Bodily-Kinesthetic Intelligence

At the end of the unit, your students are asked to "act out" what would happen to them if they had "a whole lot of air." We don't specify where all this air is. They can pantomime a person in a windstorm leaning against the wind, or an older woman trying to keep her skirt down when a gust of wind hits her. Let them make the suggestions and ask for volunteers if the suggesters don't want to pantomime the little scenes.

Developing the Mathematical-Logical Intelligence

The cause-and-effect relationships of too much air or too little air will be grasped by students who are logical thinkers. There could be an "Aha!" experience for them when they perceive that life for us and for most of the other organisms on earth can't continue without air.

Developing the Visual-Spatial Intelligence

To bring home the enormous power of air in dramatic fashion, you might show a video of a windstorm, tornado, or hurricane. All of your students will be impressed, but those who prefer to learn through the sense of sight will be especially benefited.

Developing the Interpersonal Intelligence

If a particular class discussion piques your students' interest, you might break them up into cooperative learning groups to investigate that topic. They might be especially interested in the subject of forecasting tornadoes and hurricanes, for example. Several excellent videos are available that show how scientists are trying to accurately forecast those devastating storms.

Following Through

People, animals, and plants are very vulnerable to windstorms. Wind can cause tremendous damage on land and on the water. Mountain climbers are susceptible to windstorms and blizzards, and "a whole lot of air" is a serious threat to their lives. Hot air balloons require both air and heat, and the air gets thinner the higher the balloon goes. If there is a great movement of air, balloonists have trouble controlling their crafts. Undersea divers need air to breathe and to stay underwater for long periods of time, but an overabundance of air isn't good for them. People who explore underground caves also need air, and "a whole lot of air" isn't a problem. Your students might become quite interested in massive movements of air and what causes them, especially if your area has experienced a windstorm recently. Books, films, and videos are available to help them explore the subject more fully.

A Lot of Air

When we think of air, we think of

cold air   hot air   unclean air

clean air   But most of all we think of the air we breathe.

Air is all around us. Is air everywhere? Where do we not find air?

_____

Is there air in a rock? _____ Are you sure? How do you know?

_____

Is there air in the ground? _____ How do you know?

_____

How could you find out?

_____

_____

Do liquids have air in them? _____ Which ones?

_____

_____

Would this go without air?

Would this go without air?

Would this go without air?

Would this go without air?

What other things need air to make them go? Draw pictures to show the things that need air to make them go.

Do *you* need air to make you go? _____ Why?

_____

If you had a lot of air—a whole lot of air—what would you do with it?

_____

Act out what would happen if you used all that air that way.

Unit 24

Smoke

Setting the Stage for the Unit

If your school is in or near an industrial area, you won't have to say much to set the stage for this unit. When there is an inversion, people suffer. If you are lucky enough to live in an area where smog is virtually unknown, a remark about the phenomenon and its effects on people in large cities will suffice to introduce this unit.

Administering the Unit

A few activities that can accompany Smoke are:

Developing the Naturalistic Intelligence

Smoke from fires commonly occurs in nature without the action of human beings. So we can't accuse humans alone of being responsible for smoke in the atmosphere. You can ask what smoke is and what happens to it after it forms. Smoke occurs when finely divided solid particles become mixed in a gas and become suspended in the air. The more efficiently a fire burns, the less smoke it produces.

Developing the Verbal-Linguistic and Interpersonal Intelligences

In general, we've made great progress in reducing air pollution, but the fight to clean up the air isn't over. Ask two or three of your students to look into the remaining problems concerning air pollution and give a brief report. They needn't try to read the technical material available; instead, they can interview knowledgeable people and experts (perhaps with the

> ## Smog
>
> *The word smog was first coined to describe a mixture of smoke and fog that sometimes hung over London and other cities with high humidity. The term also is used to refer to a condition caused by the action of sunlight on the exhaust gases from vehicles, factories, and homes. (In many areas there are restrictions on the use of fires outdoors and in homes.) This type of smog is called photochemical smog. Inversions—when there is a lack of air movement, with a layer of cool air near the ground and a warm layer above it— can make smog more dangerous to health.*

aid of their parents). Most large cities have scientists and technicians who constantly monitor air pollution, and their readings are often published in the daily newspaper. A group of three students would be ideal in carrying out this assignment.

Following Through

Smoke, as distinct from fire, has been useful to humans throughout the ages. Your students can follow up this unit with an investigation of smoke's uses. We can think of at least four: smoke signals, meat curing, smudge pots to protect citrus and other crops, and smoke screens.

Smoke

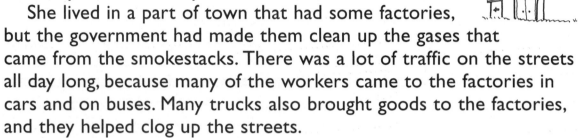

One day Lucy left her house and started walking the two blocks to her school. Then she started coughing. She noticed that the sky was darker than usual and that the air smelled bad. Lucy wondered why it was hard for her to breathe.

She lived in a part of town that had some factories, but the government had made them clean up the gases that came from the smokestacks. There was a lot of traffic on the streets all day long, because many of the workers came to the factories in cars and on buses. Many trucks also brought goods to the factories, and they helped clog up the streets.

Lucy's mother had wanted the family to move from the area because the air was bad and sometimes people were robbed. Mostly Lucy didn't mind living there, but today her nose was running and her eyes were burning. It was the air! She felt lucky that she had only two blocks to go.

What caused Lucy to cough and to have watery eyes?

_____

_____

_____

What will happen next? Finish the story.

_____

_____

_____

_____

_____

_____

Fog

Setting the Stage for the Unit

Fog is more common in some areas than in others, but if your region experiences fog fairly often in season, you'll have a chance to lead in to this unit after a foggy morning or while fog is still enveloping the school. Fog, for some of us at least, is a pleasant but mysterious atmospheric phenomenon, and we welcome its appearance. Children are sensitive to changes in the weather, and often their moods reflect this sensitivity. The unit will be of interest to many of your students, then, because it invites them to express their feelings about fog.

Administering the Unit

A few of the ways that Fog can be used to encourage the development of multiple intelligences in your students are as follows:

Developing the Mathematical-Logical Intelligence

The unit begins with a brief explanation of why fog forms. It states that fog can occur because the land or the sea (or any body of water) is cooler than the warm moisture-bearing air above it. The intellectually gifted child will have some questions about the process and will probably want more information about fog. What causes fog to "roll in," for instance? One of the most impressive sights in the San Francisco Bay area is to see the fog funnel through the Golden Gate Bridge and spread over the bay.

Developing the Intrapersonal Intelligence

Those students who are reflective will enjoy responding to the questions about how fog affects them. You might read the class Carl Sandburg's famous poem titled "Fog":

The fog comes
on little cat feet.
It sits looking
over harbor and city
on silent haunches
and then moves on.

Developing the Verbal-Linguistic Intelligence

If you read Sandburg's poem (which is very brief), this might encourage those students who enjoy verse to compose a short poem about their feelings about fog. We invite your students to do so at the end of the unit.

Developing the Bodily-Kinesthetic Intelligence

It is probably a lot to expect, but you could ask your students to use their bodies—perhaps emphasizing the hands and feet—to give a feeling of fog creeping. The student who is gifted in expressing himself in bodily movements may be able to get the idea over.

Following Through

If this unit is successful, you could follow it up with one on rain or snow. There are a number of questions you can ask to spark further learning: What is the difference between rain and fog? Is it the size of the droplets and the fact that gravity makes larger particles of water fall? By definition fog remains suspended in the air—how can the droplets stay in the air? What is *dew point*? What is the difference between a cloud and a bank of fog? These questions and many others can stimulate your students to learn more about the all-important subject of moisture in the air.

Fog

Fog forms when the land or sea cools warm air that has water in it. When the moisture in the air is cooled, it forms droplets. So to have fog, warm air must be cooled by the land or the sea.

If you have seen fog lately, where was it?

_____

_____

Are there places that don't have fog at all? _____ If so, where are they?

_____

_____

When would you like it to be very foggy?

_____

_____

What place would you like to see in a lot of fog?

_____

_____

What can you do in fog that you can't do in clear air?

_____

_____

What does it mean to "be in a fog?"

_____

_____

Would you like anyone to "be in a fog?"

_____

_____

Would you like anyone to be in a real fog? _____ If so, who?

_____

_____

Why would you like to have someone be in a real fog?

_____

_____

_____

Why don't you write a poem about fog? You can do it in the space below.

_____

_____

_____

_____

_____

_____

_____

_____

AN, HY, JU, LAW, O, PIC ✳

Unit 26

Like a Balloon

Setting the Stage for the Unit

If you want to set the stage properly for this unit, you'll blow up several balloons of varying shapes and attach them to your desk. Only two standard shapes are illustrated on the first page. Your students probably won't be terribly impressed by the balloons' presence in the room, although the balloons should cause some curiosity due to the popularity of balloon bouquets these days.

Administering the Unit

A few activities that develop multiple intelligences in your students and can be used with this unit are:

Developing the Mathematical-Logical Intelligence

This unit is a lesson in perceiving geometric shapes. Your students are asked to identify and then draw objects that look like a balloon. Unless they have had similar activities in the past, your students could be fascinated by seeing the three shapes in the large number of objects residing in your classroom. (Will anyone see the resemblance of a head to a balloon? Because of the ubiquitous Charlie Brown of Charles Schulz, it is quite possible.)

Developing the Visual-Spatial Intelligence

Your students are also asked to find objects in the shape of a tack, and this part of the unit will allow unusually perceptive youngsters to shine. A tack has two parts, and not many objects are shaped in just that way. Your students are given a third opportunity to draw in the unit—locating objects that look like a cane. This is likely the hardest of the three tasks. The cane illustrated is of the variety that has a curved

handle, but, of course, some canes don't have a curved handle.

Developing the Verbal-Linguistic Intelligence

To put into words the reasons for objects looking like a balloon or a tack or a cane, as Like a Balloon asks your students to do, is a challenging task. On the one hand, ordinary words for ordinary objects are called for; and, on the other hand, special words are required to tell how the objects resemble a balloon, tack, or cane.

Developing the Naturalistic Intelligence

A logical extension of the unit is to ask your students to name natural phenomena that are shaped like balloons, tacks, and canes. Common responses for round balloons are peas, bubbles, oak galls, pearls, melons, grapefruit, oranges, walnuts, the moon, the sun, grapes, berries, and pumpkins. Responses for tacks could be mushrooms and toadstools, trees with flattened canopies, dandelions, clover flowers, and whirlwinds. Responses for canes could be asparagus spears, icicles, stalactites, blades of grass, waterspouts, fiddlehead ferns, and horsetails. The child with an affinity for nature will probably offer several surprising items for all three shapes.

Following Through

In following up this unit, you can single out other shapes for your students to look for in the classroom and elsewhere. You might choose rectangles, squares, or triangles as the shapes to identify and draw.

Unit 26

Like a Balloon

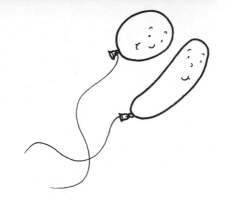

What looks like a balloon?

_____

Why do you think it looks like a balloon?

_____

Draw the way it looks.

What looks like a tack?

_____

Why do you think it looks like a tack?

_____

Draw the way it looks.

What looks like a cane?

_____

Why do you think it looks like a cane?

_____

_____

Draw the way it looks.

Balloons come in many shapes, as you know. Look hard in this room. How many things are shaped like balloons?

How many did you find? _____

Now count again. You may find some more. Did you? _____

How many more did you find? _____

Unit 27

Jacks in Space

Setting the Stage for the Unit

An ideal time to use this unit is when the media is following some space-related event such as the launch of satellites, space shuttles, rockets, or space travel. In the absence of such coverage, you can simply initiate the discussion. There should be plenty of interest in the topic, and then you can distribute Jacks in Space.

Administering the Unit

Among the many activities that can grow out of and enrich Jacks in Space are the following:

Developing the Mathematical-Logical Intelligence

The unit calls for a little knowledge of the law of gravity and its application to space travel. By this time, it wouldn't be surprising if a majority of your students already know about the problems space travelers have with weightlessness. Those who are not familiar with the condition in space vehicles can quickly learn about it if you have the class discuss the story in Jacks in Space. The students can tackle the question about what to do with the elusive ball on an individual basis.

Developing the Bodily-Kinesthetic Intelligence

There should be two or more students in your class who are willing to demonstrate how the game of jacks is played. You need only provide the jacks and ball.

Developing the Verbal-Linguistic Intelligence

This unit offers an opportunity for students to exhibit and expand their vocabularies. If enough interest is generated, you can provide information (at the appropriate reading levels) about space travel, and/or your students can find books and other materials in the library or on the Internet.

Developing the Interpersonal Intelligence

If there is sufficient interest to look into the problem posed in the unit (or related problems), your students can be split up into groups of four or five to gather more information and make hypotheses.

Developing the Naturalistic Intelligence

The individuals in your class who have an inclination to observe natural phenomena can cite instances where gravity controls what we can and can't do on Earth.

Developing the Visual-Spatial Intelligence

Those students who are good at drawing might try to show a solution to the problem with a drawing or diagram.

Following Through

Jacks in Space can kick off a unit of study concerning gravity and space travel, or a unit just on gravity. The unit could be oriented toward solving problems such as the effects of gravity on eating, moving, sleeping, exercising muscles, and more.

Jacks in Space

Let's imagine that you live in a large spaceship. You have lived in the spaceship for six months. Being in a spaceship is fun. There is a lot to do, but you have to keep remembering that things aren't the same as on Earth. If you flip a coin, it won't fall back into your hand. Why won't the coin fall back into your hand?

_____

_____

_____

_____

Once you tried to play jacks. The steel jacks were easy to throw, because you threw them on a pad. Why did the jacks stick to the pad?

_____

_____

_____

_____

But the rubber ball kept floating away when you bounced it. Why did the ball keep floating away?

_____

_____

_____

Learning from Nature © 2005 • www.zephyrpress.com

Since you like to play jacks very much, you try to think of how not to lose the ball all the time. How can you stop the ball from floating away from you when you bounce it?

_____

_____

_____

_____

_____

Unit 28

Bubbles

Setting the Stage for the Unit

Little children enjoy blowing bubbles. Nowadays, they can make huge ones, almost as big as themselves. You could introduce this unit by bringing to class a ring or pipe, along with the appropriate liquid, and blowing a few bubbles. Adults secretly enjoy blowing bubbles, too, although they rarely do so when not in the company of children.

Administering the Unit

A few of the activities that might accompany the administration of Bubbles are:

Developing the Naturalistic Intelligence

The dictionary definition of a bubble is "a film of liquid forming a ball of air or gas." Bubbles occur in nature in countless situations. Consequently, we see bubbles at the ocean's edge, at fountains and waterfalls, and when we pour milk. Your students will be very much aware of the formation of bubbles in all of these situations and many, many more.

One or more of your students may volunteer that a baby brother or sister can make bubbles (and that the student can, too!). You can have your students perform a very simple experiment, in which they mix liquids of different consistencies in separate pans to see if there are differences in the amount of bubbles produced when they stir them.

Developing the Verbal-Linguistic and Mathematical-Logical Intelligences

If you have your students perform the little experiment, ask them to express their findings in words and, if possible, numbers. (For example, "The pan with soap and water had about twice as many bubbles as the pan with water and vinegar.")

Following Through

You can ask your students if the foam at the top of a root beer float is only a conglomeration of bubbles. If so, where did the air (oxygen) come from? You might demonstrate with a root beer or any other carbonated beverage and find out if the children know what "carbonated" (CO_2) means. How does the beverage acquire its carbonation? What happens when you store a half-empty bottle without capping it?

Bubbles

Have you ever blown soap bubbles? _____

What do you like best about blowing bubbles?

_____

_____

Do you like to pop them? _____ Why or why not?

_____

_____

Have you blown any other kinds of bubbles? _____ What kind?

_____

What is the difference between blowing soap bubbles and blowing other kinds of bubbles?

_____

_____

When water boils, you see bubbles coming to the surface and popping. Why does this happen?

_____

_____

If you splash in the water, you'll see some bubbles near the surface. What causes the bubbles to form?

_____

_____

What is a bubble, anyway?

_____

When do we see bubbles?

_____

_____

What things look like bubbles but aren't made of air and water?

_____

_____

_____

What happens when these things have bubbles?

1. gum _____

2. hot cereal _____

3. a baby _____

4. pottery _____

5. glass _____

6. varnish _____

7. a blood vessel _____

Draw a picture of what happens when one of the things just mentioned has bubbles.

Draw a picture showing what happens next. Give your picture enough detail so that anyone can tell what happens next.

Unit 29

Sky Watch

Setting the Stage for the Unit

This is a unit that the students do on their own. They choose the time and place to look at the sky or at trees. What your students will see when they look up at the sky for half an hour is hard to predict. If a child looks on a cloudy day, there will be mostly clouds, but it also is likely that the child will see birds and possibly aircraft. In industrial areas there might be smoke. The important point about the activity is that the students keep looking for a full half-hour. You'll want to consult the weather forecasts and choose a day for sky watching that promises fairly good weather before you give the assignment.

Administering the Unit

A few of the ways that you can encourage the development of your students' multiple intelligences follow:

Developing the Naturalistic Intelligence

This unit is designed to serve two purposes. First, your students will notice, perhaps for the first time, phenomena in their world, such as cloud formations or holes in trees. Second, children who are curious about nature will likely enjoy the opportunity to do some uninterrupted observing. The title of the unit is Sky Watch, but it may be just as rewarding for your students to study whatever trees they can find in the area.

If the sky is completely overcast and unchanging, some students might welcome the chance to look at trees. They might be able to identify some of the species that they see and, perhaps, differentiate between those that are deciduous and those that are evergreen. Most of the children who look at trees instead of the sky will probably also notice birds. Upon very close inspection, the nature lovers may detect animals such as squirrels and insects as well.

Developing the Verbal-Linguistic Intelligence

The unit has your students recording on paper the phenomena that they observe, and this will be a strain on their vocabularies. Some of the students might show a little consternation, but this unit will provide them with the opportunity to acquire a vocabulary relevant to various cloud formations and how they are formed, and to learn the names of specific trees, birds, and insects. The child who is keenly interested in nature or in acquiring words for his vocabulary will take advantage of this opportunity.

Developing the Visual-Spatial Intelligence

If a child is talented at drawing, it will be natural for him or her to sketch a cloud formation, tree, or bird. Encourage any children who wish to add drawings to their account of what they observed.

Following Through

If the conditions are right, the logical follow-up activity for Sky Watch is to have your students look at the sky at night. Some of the children may already know something about the planets and stars, and perhaps the Milky Way. Since humankind has been to the moon and explored space, a little of the mystery has gone out of gazing at the planets and stars even as a good deal of adventure has been added. Your students might be amazed by the spectacle, even though they have rarely gazed intently at the heavens, or vice versa. Playing with toys that are inspired by *Star Wars*–type films is not the same kind of thinking and imagining as trying to identify constellations in the sky. Sky Watch encourages observational and contemplative thinking.

Children should ask adults to accompany them when they look at the sky at night.

Sky Watch

Go outside and look at the sky. If there are any clouds, keep looking at the sky for half an hour. Write down what you see. Don't write just one thing. Write down as many things as you can.

If there are no clouds in the sky, find some trees. Look at the trees for half an hour. Write down as many things about the trees as you can see. Don't write just one or two things on your paper. Use the space on the left side of the paper below.

Now imagine what the weather will be like a year from now. On the same day and at the same time of day, what will the sky or trees look like next year? Will the sky or the trees look the same? Is the weather always the same on the same date of the year?

Write your guesses on the right side of the paper.

What you saw this year   What you will see next year

_____   _____

_____   _____

_____   _____

_____   _____

_____   _____

_____   _____

_____   _____

Unit 30

It's Hot!

Setting the Stage for the Unit

The best time to administer this unit is when the weather is either quite hot or quite cold. It would also be a good idea to administer it when the children are alert but not silly. The lesson is comprised of only four questions concerning four unusual instruments. You can introduce it by asking, "Have you ever heard someone say, 'I can't believe my eyes!'? Well, you are about to see some things that might make you say something like that."

Administering the Unit

The following are a few activities that can be administered in conjunction with It's Hot!:

Developing the Naturalistic Intelligence

For the children who follow weather reports, the thermometer registering 185°F will seem unreal. That temperature isn't unusual in an oven, of course—it would be rather cool—but most of your students will assume that it is an outdoor thermometer. You can ask what the record high temperatures are for the community and for the state; one or two of your students may know, and you can easily find out if you don't know the answers. Professional meteorologists are found in most areas.

Developing the Mathematical-Logical Intelligence

You can ask your students to look in the newspaper to learn what the high temperature was for the day, and then compare it with the 185°F indicated on the thermometer in the unit. Then you can lead a discussion about what differences we feel when it is 70°F as compared to 80°F or 90°F. When the temperature is 100°F it seems a great deal hotter than 90°F and 105°F is stifling to most people. A brief comment can be made about how humidity affects our comfort level.

Following Through

Ask your students if they know why most of our rulers are twelve inches long. It is unlikely that they know the historical reasons for the English system of measurement. (For your able readers, the history is readily available in encyclopedias.) They will have probably seen measurements in the metric system, so you can give them a brief overview of the advantages of the metric system over the English system.

It's Hot!

What would you think if you saw this?

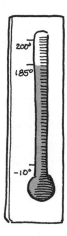

_____

_____

_____

_____

What would you think if you saw a clock like this?

_____

_____

_____

_____

What would you think if you saw this ruler?

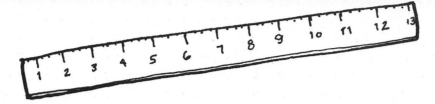

_____

_____

_____

What would you think if you saw this sign?

_____

_____

_____

Unit 31

Floating Round

Setting the Stage for the Unit

This unit can logically follow Bubbles (Unit 28) inasmuch as balloons are compared with bubbles in the unit. A balloon shares two of a bubble's chief characteristics: it is usually spherical and full of air. You can lead into the lesson with a remark about hot air balloons or balloons filled with helium that escape into the atmosphere. (There have been complaints that they are hazardous to birds, sea life, and possibly aircraft.)

Administering the Unit

A few of the activities that can be administered in conjunction with Floating Round are:

Developing the Naturalistic Intelligence

Smaller balloons have become more commercial in recent years because of two customs: retailers have started combining them in bunches and sending them as bouquets, and people have begun using them to note the location of a party or some event. Larger balloons—hot air balloons—have been in the news for many years, because of the adventurers who fly in them over oceans, mountains, and other difficult terrain. Accordingly, your students are quite familiar with balloons. Most of them will have had the experience of blowing them up. Unlike bubbles, balloons don't occur naturally. They are man-made and, therefore, might not always be ecologically beneficial. Ask your students to explain when balloons are harmful to the environment.

Developing the Visual-Spatial Intelligence

Your students' principal task in this unit is to draw *bright* balloons. Encourage them to use bright colors so their drawings will make an attractive display, showing off their collective brilliance.

Developing the Verbal-Linguistic and Interpersonal Intelligences

You might suggest that your students get together in small groups and collaborate on composing a story about the adventures of a balloon. When they have decided on the story's main events and worked it up into a finished story, they can present it as a skit (perhaps with a balloon as a prop).

Following Through

If you and your students enjoy crafts, balloons can be the foundation for attractive sculpture-like objects that are covered with paper and paste and then painted in colorful designs. The results can be satisfying.

Unit 31

Floating Round

What do you think of balloons? Do you like them? _____ Why or why not?

_____

_____

Is anything that floats in the air like a balloon?

_____

Is a bubble a balloon? _____ Why or why not?

_____

_____

Name some things that look like balloons.

_____

_____

_____

What makes a balloon a balloon?

_____

_____

_____

Whenever Ann thinks about balloons, she thinks of bright balloons. What might those balloons look like? Why don't you draw some?

Whenever Jim thinks about balloons, he thinks of the kind with funny shapes. What might they look like?

What do we use balloons for?

_____

_____

_____

Draw a picture of the kind of balloon you like best.

Learning from Nature © 2005 • www.zephyrpress.com

Unit 32

Come Back

Setting the Stage for the Unit

The concept of this unit is that of returning. Along with waiting, humankind does a lot of returning. In many ways we return every day—to our homes, workplaces, chores, bad habits, unfinished books and letters, favorite chairs and sofas, as well as to our favorite ongoing sitcoms, scenes of our childhood, our everyday hassles, and even, in the event of a lapse of sensibility, to our senses. There is no end to our returning. For your students, a remark or two such as "Let's get back to work" (after a long diversion) can serve to introduce this unit. The children will quickly grasp the concept if you also remark that "We do a lot of getting back, as happens in this lesson."

Administering the Unit

The following activities can accompany the administration of Come Back:

Developing the Naturalistic Intelligence

The answers to the first three questions are obvious (unless a child is not familiar with a boomerang). The concept of returning is further developed when your students are asked to name some animals that return daily and some that return after six months or more. Most animals have a place in which they sleep, rest, seek refuge, bear young, and so forth. Among the ones that come readily to mind are bees, ants, birds, rabbits, squirrels, and foxes. Some animals, however, roam over their territories and establish a rude place for sleeping every night. The gorilla is such a creature, and of course, so are migrating animals when they are on the move. You shouldn't have to hint too broadly to help the youngsters answer these two questions. They should be aware of the daily returners, such as the bees, ants, burrowing animals, nesting birds, and cows. They also should think of salmon, swallows ("When the swallows come back to Capistrano"), caribou, gray whales, and other animals that return to certain areas because of instincts or the availability of food.

Developing the Verbal-Linguistic Intelligence

Any of the animals that the children cite in the last part of the unit could provide a good discussion. One or more of your students, if motivated, might want to make an oral report on the gray whale, salmon, swallow, squirrel, gopher, or some other interesting animal.

Developing the Visual-Spatial Intelligence

The burrowing animals are fascinating to study because they have underground passageways that lead to emergency exits, and that contain chambers for sleeping, rearing young, and storing food. If you have a youngster who is good at drawing and is adept at perceiving spatial relationships, she or he might want to make a diagram of a prairie dog's burrow. Prairie dogs are especially interesting because they make alterations as they live in their burrows, plugging and unplugging entrances and digging tunnels and new rooms.

Following Through

It goes without saying that there are a great many beautifully illustrated books for young children about wildlife. You should have no trouble finding these treasures and showing them to your class.

Come Back

What does this do when you throw it?

_____

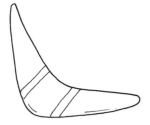

When you haven't seen it for a long time, what does this do in the spring?

_____

_____

What happens after water changes to vapor and becomes a cloud?

_____

_____

Each of the pictures shows something that can *return* to where it was, or to the way it was. This is the way with many things. There are fishes that always return to the same place to lay their eggs. Some birds travel thousands of miles in the fall, but they always return in the spring to the nesting grounds where they were born. Even such huge animals as whales return to the same waters where they were born when it is time to calf.

Can you think of a *sound* that comes back?

_____

_____

What large sea animal squeaks so that it can tell how far away objects are?

_____

What winged animal does the same thing so that it won't bump into anything?

_____

Keep track of all the things you can see today that *return* to where they started from, or to the way they were. You can write their names here.

_____

_____

_____

_____

_____

_____

_____

_____

Unit 33

More Than Music

Setting the Stage for the Unit

Inasmuch as the sight and sound of bells are part of every child's experience, you might introduce More Than Music by asking a question such as "What is your favorite kind of bell?" or "Most people like bells—what kind of bells do you like?" You might be able to anticipate most of the responses to your question, but a few could surprise you. Your students may never have thought of a bell as anything but an instrument for summoning people. Therefore, a brief discussion of different kinds of bells will help prepare them for thinking in depth about this marvelous invention of man. Having a bell on your desk, especially if you use one regularly, would be a good idea. If bells ring at your school to begin and end the school day or for fire drills, your students can discuss these signals also.

Administering the Unit

Following are only a few ideas for using More Than Music to encourage the development of multiple intelligences:

Developing the Musical-Rhythmical Intelligence

It would be well if you had a bell with which to demonstrate when administering this unit. Any kind of bell will do; however, if one of your students volunteers that he or she has heard a hand bell rung in a bell choir, a hand bell could be used to show that a single note can be produced from a bell. (Of course, there are overtones, as there are in producing notes from other instruments.) The bell you have for demonstration purposes can be either shaken or struck in various ways. Rapid ringing, rhythmic ringing, slow ringing, and even syncopated ringing can be

demonstrated by you or a musical student. It will be easy for your students to sense urgency in the rapid ringing. How do wedding bells sound? What makes them sound happy?

Developing the Verbal-Linguistic Intelligence

The unit begins with the statement that an ordinary bell has "many, many uses." It is quite possible that this thought will be entirely new to several of your students. They might not connect a bell with music, alarms, time, rejoicing, or locating an animal such as a cow, but they might well associate a bell with recess and dinner. However, as a result of their listing all the uses they can think of for bells, your students will begin to understand that bells are indeed versatile and valuable devices.

Next, the student is asked to think of another object or device that has as many uses as a bell. If you administer this unit orally to your class, this question could be the kick-off for an amazing intellectual excursion—or it could be the barrier to further exploration. Without providing too many cues, encourage your students to search their minds for reasonable answers to this question. It is important—and this is the difficult part—that the children be able to back up their responses with solid reasoning and sufficient evidence. Your job is to see that they understand that they must have support for their answers. And this must be accomplished without their feeling foolish or stupid. In other words, they should not feel punished for responding to the question.

After they have done a good deal of thinking about bells, their forms, and their uses, the children are issued an invitation to write a story or a poem about a bell. Notice that the students are invited to write. If they are not interested in the subject, they should not be forced to produce a story or verse in a half-hearted manner. Children who have a talent for writing won't have to be coaxed.

Developing the Mathematical-Logical Intelligence

The musically talented student may also be gifted in mathematics and reasoning. (For a good reason, mathematicians love to play Bach and perform in string quartets.) That youngster might be able to explain intervals and the value of full-notes, half-notes, and quarter-notes.

Developing the Naturalistic Intelligence

Are there any bell-like sounds in nature? Perhaps the closest are sounds made by birds. Water and wind ordinarily don't cause bell-like sounds, and neither do most animals. The child who knows and loves nature may have some thoughts about this question.

Developing the Intrapersonal Intelligence

After ringing your bell, you can ask, "What does the bell ringing make you think of?" and "How does that sound make you feel?" The responses might be written down so that the children do not influence one another.

Developing the Interpersonal Intelligence

If, by chance, you have several students who have experience playing in bell choirs, they can play a tune for the class after working out the details of the performance. Performing in a bell choir requires a lot of teamwork.

Following Through

More Than Music could be a rough model for similar exercises that you can devise to meet the particular needs of your students. We are certain that you will be able to think of many concepts or objects to explore with the children, but here are three that might possibly prove suitable for your class.

Bubbles are fascinating to children, so you might ask your students to think of occasions when they see bubbles form. Since bubble baths are still popular these days, many will surely think of a bathtub as a place where bubbles occur. They should also think of the soap bubbles that are produced with the aid of a pipe or wire (and the kind that need nothing more than a tongue and a supply of saliva); but they may or may not think of the foam along the seashore, the bubbles in a carbonated drink, or the bubbles that signify boiling water. A few of the children might also remember the bubbles at a geyser. Why do we have bubbles? What is inside a bubble? Is it *always* air?

Locks are frequently of great interest to young people. There are all kinds of locks, of course, and it should be easy for you and your students to think of the various ways people have of locking things in, out, and up. Those students who have unusual locks and keys should be encouraged to bring them to class. Very often, the keys to locks are especially fascinating. Museums have wonderful collections of locks, and your class might follow up their discussion with a visit to a nearby museum.

Rings may fascinate your students, and they also can serve as objects to study. The rings that the children are probably most familiar with are those for the fingers and the ears. The circle that a ring makes has a symbolic meaning, and you could explore that a little with your students. Is a circle the sign of perfection? Immortality? Unity? Some of your students may know of rings other than those fashioned for hands or ears. There are rings for the noses of bulls, doughnuts, rings on posts for tying up horses, onion rings, rings on bollards (or posts) for tying up boats and ships, rings for linking ropes and chains, rings to be grabbed when on a merry-go-round, rings of growth in trees, and so on.

There are a great number of objects that might be explored, of course. Those that have particular relevance for units of study are probably ones that you will find most profitable to investigate in depth.

One of the purposes of this unit is to help students develop their ability to look at something familiar in greater depth. It may be used to introduce a lesson in art or some other field.

More than Music

This is a bell.

It is just a common bell, but it is really quite wonderful. It has many, many uses. How many different ways can a bell be used? Write them in the spaces below.

_____

_____

_____

_____

_____

Can you think of anything else that has as many uses as a bell? What is it?

_____

What are some of the ways it can be used?

_____

_____

_____

_____

Why don't you write a story about a bell? Or maybe you would prefer to write a poem. If you write a poem, you could put it to music.

Unit 34

Waking Up

Setting the Stage for the Unit

Since your students all have the same experience every morning–namely, that of waking up from sleep–they have something in common that you can use to lead into this unit. You can ask them if it is easy or hard for them to get up and whether they get up with the help of another person or with some kind of alarm. There seem to be two types of individuals when it comes to waking up in the morning, and usually they are that way all through their lifetimes. One type finds it very difficult to awaken (characterized by Dagwood in *Blondie*), and another type bounces out of bed wide awake. Your students undoubtedly fall roughly into those two groups and might enjoy talking about their first chore of the day.

Administering the Unit

A few activities that give students various opportunities to develop their multiple intelligences and that can be administered with Waking Up are:

Developing the Intrapersonal Intelligence

You could ask your students whether they are aware of the reasons why it is easy or hard for them to get up in the morning. Is it hard because of the time at which they got to sleep? Is it hard because of the conditions of the bed and room in which they sleep? Does it depend upon the kind of sleep they've had (bad dreams, good dreams, disturbed sleep)?

Developing the Mathematical-Logical Intelligence

The unit has several points where the students have to get an answer to a question by subtracting. This unit provides a chance for you to introduce or review the notations we make for time (3:00 A.M., 5:12 P.M., etc.). You might tell your students what A.M. and P.M. mean.

Developing the Naturalistic Intelligence

The child who knows about birds or is a light sleeper might be able to tell fairly accurately the times at which birds start chirping in the morning. It depends upon the time of year, of course, and the weather often is a factor. We've known birds to chirp at 4:00 A.M. Some birds start singing before others, and your students can have fun discussing the "early birds" and then doing some research to see if they are correct.

Developing the Verbal-Linguistic Intelligence

Waking Up encourages your students to express themselves orally and in writing. The students who love to express themselves in words will enjoy talking and writing about the universal experience of waking up from sleep.

Developing the Bodily-Kinesthetic Intelligence

Some of your students might want to pantomime what happens when they have to get up in the morning.

Developing the Interpersonal Intelligence

You might have two or three youngsters perform a skit about getting up in the morning. Skits offer children chances to develop skills of leadership and cooperative planning. The students have to assign roles and then carry them out in an organized way. A tape recorder will help them to evaluate their progress as they work things out.

Developing the Musical-Rhythmical Intelligence

One or more of the "naturalist" students in your class may be able to imitate the songs of the avian early risers. You can point out the rhythmic patterns that distinguish birdcalls. If you are lucky enough to have mockingbirds in your area, listening to a mocker is a lesson in showing how rhythm plays as big, or bigger, a part as pitch in a bird's song.

Following Through

A natural follow-up activity for Waking Up is to ask your students to note the time they wake up the morning after you administer this unit. The times can be arrayed on the chalkboard; and, although you probably won't want to give the statistical names for the averages, you can point out the mean (arithmetic average), mode (most frequent) time, and the median (the time at which half of the times of awakening fall below and half of them above). It could be that two of these measures of central tendency are the same, because the children's schedules are constrained by the time they have to get to school. The activity should be interesting to them, because they will be curious about when their classmates have to get up. Some students may surprise you as well as their classmates by revealing how little time they take from arising until arriving at school.

Unit 34

Waking Up

Some birds get up very early in the morning. Guess which bird gets up first in the morning and sings. _____

How can you find out if you are right?

_____

_____

Guess the time when that bird gets up. _____

When do *you* get up? _____

How long before you are up does that bird get up?

_____

What does that bird do before you get up? Tell all about what birds do in the morning.

_____

_____

_____

_____

Find out when others in your family get up. Then find out how much earlier that "early bird" is up than each member of your family.

_____

_____

_____

_____

_____

Would You Rather Be a Mouse?

Setting the Stage for the Unit

If your room contains a mouse or a rat (as an invited guest), this unit might be a "natural" for encouraging your students to develop their expressional and empathic abilities. Even if all of them choose to be a mouse, your students will undoubtedly perceive the life of a mouse a bit differently, and they will express these perceptions in diverse ways. The role of the piglet might be favored by children in a rural area, especially since mice do a good deal of damage to grain and other supplies. The majority of students who encounter this unit, however, will be from urban and suburban homes, and they may have only limited knowledge of a mouse and none whatsoever of a piglet. It could be profitable, particularly for children from urban and suburban areas, to investigate their conceptions and misconceptions about pigs and mice before you administer the unit.

Administering the Unit

There follow some ideas for using this unit to help develop your students' multiple intelligences:

Developing the Intrapersonal Intelligence

This unit is definitely a matter of individuals responding to the questions and invitations, and thus we recommend that you have each child do it on his or her own. The personification device is used to cause your students to give more than a cursory thought to the two familiar animals. Those that are more introspective will have a chance to consider what it is like to be an animal and, in contrast, also what it is like to be a young person.

Developing the Naturalistic Intelligence

Some of your students may know a good deal about pigs or mice. This unit affords gives them an opportunity to share their knowledge, and this sharing could be the highlight of the activity.

Developing the Mathematical-Logical Intelligence

After asking your students whether they would prefer being a piglet or a mouse, we force them to back up their choices with a reason. "Are you sure?" we ask, and then we follow up that question by asking, "Why (would you rather be one than the other)?" A student's first response may be somewhat superficial, but the questions that follow concerning the desirability of being a mouse or a piglet in a storm or in the city or on a train will cause her to think more deeply. Countless other questions can be asked, of course, and you may want to supplement the questions in the unit with a few of your own. Here are several that might easily have been included in the unit:

Which one would you rather be—a mouse or a piglet:

* in an apartment house?
* on Friday?
* at nighttime?
* on Christmas Eve?
* in an airplane?
* on a ship?
* in a theater?

The question about the relative longevity of the animals is not touched upon, but there may be a realist in your class who will think about the ultimate fate of the piglet (most should have read *Charlotte's Web* by now) and the brief lifespan of a mouse.

Developing the Verbal-Linguistic Intelligence

The students are asked for a number of responses in the unit, and some students will tend to offer brief responses that are not thought through. Verbally adept students will be able to answer the questions and to explain the reasoning for their answers with an adequate vocabulary and correct spelling, syntax, and grammar.

Developing the Musical-Rhythmical Intelligence

The section of this unit that might appeal most to your students has to do with their singing and dancing like mice and piglets. (We believe that Walt Disney made use of singing mice, but your class may be doing some important pioneering in the field of singing pigs.) You should have a good deal of fun with this unit.

Developing the Visual-Spatial Intelligence

For those youngsters who learn best when their eyes are taking in information, you might supplement the illustrations with prints or photographs of mice and young pigs in their natural surroundings. (In the case of a mouse, that could be almost anywhere.) As a subject for a drawing, either would be unusual, but for this unit it would be natural to ask the students to draw one of the reasons they prefer to be one or the other.

Following Through

It has probably occurred to you that the format of Would You Rather Be a Mouse? could be used to introduce regular curricular units. You will have no trouble adapting the basic idea of this unit to one in science, health, history, or geography. Any pair of alternatives can be substituted for the piglet and the mouse. Just one word of caution: before submitting the questions to your class, it is a good idea to think through the implication of each question you plan to use.

Would You Rather Be a Mouse?

Would you rather be a mouse

or a piglet? _____

Are you sure? _____ Why?

_____

_____

_____

Even in a storm? _____

Or in the city? _____

Or on a train? _____

Show how you would be a mouse or a piglet—
by singing about what you would do,
by dancing like a mouse or a piglet,
or by drawing what might happen to you if you were a piglet or a
mouse.

Unit 36

You Can't See Me

Setting the Stage for the Unit

This unit is about hiding: the sun hides, the moon hides, the student hides, and even toys hide. It should appeal to youngsters. There are any number of ways to lead in to You Can't See Me, but probably the most effective would be to hide an object and then challenge your students to find it. You could hide the object (not too small nor too big) in the classroom—but in plain sight. That is, it would be visible but not obvious. The students could remain in their seats and try to spot it.

Administering the Unit

A few of the ways You Can't See Me can be used to encourage your students to develop their multiple intelligences are:

Developing the Verbal-Linguistic Intelligence

After reflecting about the diversions of hiding, your students are invited to write a story in which someone hides. They aren't told if the character is discovered or not, so there should be a great variety of plots for their stories. Since there have been so many films based on this theme, we hope that your students aren't unduly influenced by Indiana Jones and his imitators.

Developing the Naturalistic Intelligence

Some of your students may take a realistic view of the text in You Can't See Me. We aren't able to see much of anything without sufficient light. The child who is aware of the constant changes in the atmosphere and in the living things that inhabit his world will offer sound explanations for the questions

about hiding. Certainly a great many animals hide, and they must be good at it, too, in order to survive.

Developing the Visual-Spatial Intelligence

If a student is eager to illustrate his or her story, you should allot time for that activity. The illustration will add to the attractiveness and meaning of the story and give the artistically gifted child a chance to develop his or her talents further.

Developing the Intrapersonal Intelligence

There are several questions concerning the student's personal experiences with hiding. Where is her own private place? Do any of her toys seem to hide from her? Does she prefer hiding or seeking? This unit should strike a chord with those children who have active imaginations.

Developing the Bodily-Kinesthetic Intelligence

The game of hide-and-seek is mentioned toward the beginning of the unit, and, depending upon the age of your students, you might ask for volunteers to tell about their favorite hiding places and show what postures they use when hiding.

Following Through

The stories written (and illustrated) by the children can be displayed and/or bound together. You will want the children to make sure that their productions are as neat and correct in spelling, punctuation, and grammar as they can make them.

After discussing hide-and-seek, your students may might want to play the game under your supervision on the playground.

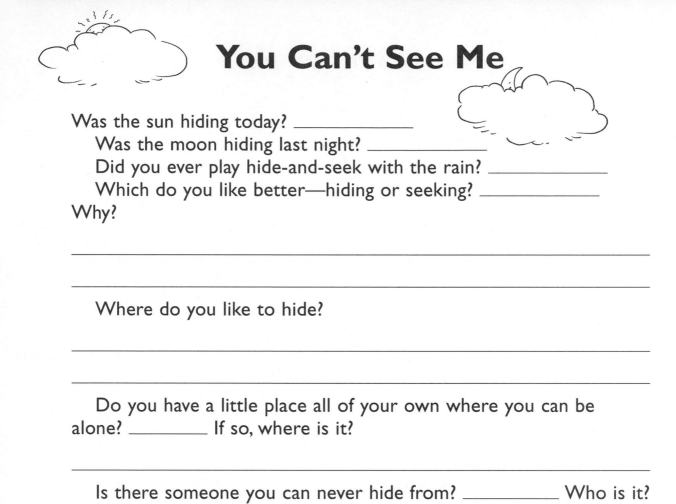

You Can't See Me

Was the sun hiding today? _____

    Was the moon hiding last night? _____

    Did you ever play hide-and-seek with the rain? _____

    Which do you like better—hiding or seeking? _____
Why?

_____

_____

    Where do you like to hide?

_____

_____

    Do you have a little place all of your own where you can be alone? _____ If so, where is it?

_____

    Is there someone you can never hide from? _____ Who is it?

_____

    Do you know an animal that likes to hide? _____ What is it?

_____

    Does anyone in your family like to hide? _____ If so, who is it?

_____

    Write a story about somebody who hides or something that is hidden. You can jot down your ideas on the back of this handout.

Unit 37

Kings and Queens

Setting the Stage for the Unit

With the possible exception of our pets, animals don't care what we call them. The names we give wild animals are only for our sake, to help us identify them. To lead into the unit you might ask your students if they know why the lion is called "The King of Beasts." Since a lion isn't as big or powerful as an elephant, shouldn't the elephant be called "The King of Beasts"?

Administering the Unit

The following are activities that can accompany the administration of Kings and Queens:

Developing the Naturalistic Intelligence

This unit calls for some knowledge of living things. Your students are asked to name an insect, a fish, a reptile, and a bird that deserve to be called "king," "prince," or "queen." If they simply pick the largest or most familiar creature, they won't be thinking very deeply. A whale, for example, can't be called "The King of Fishes" because it is a mammal. If the children nominate a snake as "The Prince of Reptiles," ask them to specify which snake. (There is, of course, a king snake.)

Developing the Bodily-Kinesthetic Intelligence

Does the alpha male of a pack of wolves "carry himself" differently than do the other males in the pack? Does a dominant horse in a herd of wild horses deport himself differently than the other stallions? If your students are aware of these characteristics of the leaders of social animals, one or more might pantomime how certain animals show their dominance by the movements of their bodies.

Following Through

There can be follow-up questions of the same kind as the ones in this unit:

* What animal might be called "The King of Amphibians"?
* What animal could be called "The Queen of the Barnyard"?
* What animal might be called "The Prince of the Forest"?
* Which animal is the "Emperor of Pets"?

Kings and Queens

We call the lion "The King of Beasts." When you hear the lion called that, you get the idea that he bosses the other animals around. Except for the elephant and a few others, that's true.

Have you thought about giving royal names to other animals? It seems right that some other animals should have names that suit their size, strength, or brains.

Which fish should be called "King of the Fishes"? _____ Why?

_____

_____

Which bird should be called "Princess of the Birds"? _____ Why?

_____

_____

Which reptile should be called "Prince of the Reptiles"?

_____

Why? _____

_____

Sometimes a dog is named "King" and a cat is called "Queenie." Why would a dog be named "King"?

_____

_____

_____

Unit 38

Pinecone or Orchid?

Setting the Stage for the Unit

Every child engages in the kind of imaginative activity we call personification, and so your students should be able to imagine that they are orchids and pinecones without too much difficulty. On the other hand, the idea that fantasy is a legitimate classroom activity seems unusual to many students and teachers. Actually, a child's powers of reasoning and relating can be developed through the agency of fantasy.

This unit can lead into investigations of forest conservation, tropical plants, and the formation of seeds and therefore might be included in many social studies and science units. Since the student's decision as to whether to be a pinecone or an orchid is challenged by a series of questions in the unit, she or he will have to consider each object in more than one light. Accordingly, the student will be encouraged to learn more about these two wonders of nature.

Administering the Unit

Teachers of primary-grade children often prefer to present this type of exercise orally, and there are some distinct advantages to that method of presentation. The children can benefit from each other's thinking (in the same manner as they would by the "hitchhiking" that takes place in a brainstorming session). For most classes, however, we recommend that you have the children respond to the questions both orally and in writing. This can be accomplished by having the children read through the exercise and respond to the questions on their own. Then ask some of the students to read the questions aloud for their classmates to answer. At this point, you can encourage an interplay of ideas.

The following activities can be administered with the unit:

Developing the Naturalistic and Verbal-Linguistic Intelligences

After the children have done their imagining about pinecones and orchids, they are invited to make up a poem or song about the forest, flowers, or one of the seasons. A haiku is a type of verse that, traditionally, expresses the author's feelings about the seasons and nature. Although haiku is a little advanced for second- and third-grade students, it has been used successfully with younger students and is meant to express feelings about the seasons and nature. As you probably know, haiku consists of only three lines of five, seven, and five syllables, respectively. It isn't important that the syllabication pattern is followed exactly. An excellent and inexpensive reference is *The Classic Tradition of Haiku*, an anthology edited by Faubion Bowers (Dover Thrift, 1996).

After pretending to be pinecones or orchids, your students might then dig into the intimate details about the natural environment, basic nature, uses, and the like of the two things. Then you can ask the children to personify pinecones and orchids a second time, and you will be able to study the difference that information makes in an individual's ability to empathize, or to feel, with something else.

Following Through

You may receive some surprises when you learn which children prefer being a pinecone and which choose to be an orchid. It might be supposed that girls would invariably identify with the flower, for example, but there may be one or more young girls in your class who will see themselves as pinecones. The reasons for the choices are more important than the choices themselves, of course. A child may see the pinecone as an instrument for recreation, and this

93

tells us something about the way he or she thinks. Another student may see an orchid as an object that brings beauty into our lives and gives us pleasure; this kind of reasoning also gives us an indication of the child's experiences and his or her approach to life. It may be that one of your students will think of a pinecone in terms of food (pine nuts are popular with children in some parts of the country). Others may find it extremely difficult to decide at all; this inability to solve the dilemma can itself be most revealing.

If you discover topics of particular interest to the students while administering this exercise, we suggest that you encourage them to investigate the subjects on their own. The entire class could become quite inter-ested in orchids, conifers, epiphytes, pollination, cross-fertilization, or some other topic; the result could be an unscheduled but rewarding unit of study.

You certainly could use this format on other occasions, if you see a purpose in doing so. Questions such as "Would you rather be a pelican or a her-ring?" could point to important topics in a unit about marine life. "Would you rather be a moth or a butterfly?" is a question that could lead to some interesting findings if your class were studying Lepidoptera or about insects more generally. Of course, none of these questions is worth the trouble if you do not also ask your students to give sound rea-sons for their choices.

Pinecone or Orchid?

Would you rather be a pinecone or an orchid? _____ Why?

_____

_____

What does a pinecone do?

_____

_____

Can an orchid do the same things? _____

Would you like to be a pinecone in the summer? _____ Why?

_____

_____

_____

Or would you rather be an orchid in the summer? _____

Why? _____

_____

_____

_____

Which would you rather be in the winter—a pinecone or an orchid? _____

Why? _____

_____

Would you enjoy making up a poem or a song about the forest, flowers, or one of the seasons? Why don't you draw a picture that tells about your poem or song?

_____

_____

_____

_____

_____

_____

   Learning from Nature © 2005 • www.zephyrpress.com

In Your Hands

Setting the Stage for the Unit

This unit is about one of the most important and fascinating subjects concerning humankind, the hands. To set the stage for the unit, you might simply compare your hands with a student's hands. Ask: "Who can hold more in his or her hands? What allows us to grasp things in our hands? In general, is it easier to hold live things in your hands or inanimate things?"

You also might call attention to the countless ways we use our hands, and then mention the role the thumb has played in the evolution of humans as tool-using creatures. Unquestionably, the subject of hands can lead to any number of adventures in learning, but the unit itself is only concerned with what human hands can hold.

Administering the Unit

Following are a few of the activities that can be administered with In Your Hands in order to increase learning in your students:

Developing the Bodily-Kinesthetic Intelligence

Touching is a way of finding out, of knowing. In some cultures it is more common and important than in ours, but all young children seem to want to touch, and a great deal of early learning is accomplished through the sense of touch. We have little zoos for petting animals and pools in aquariums for touching marine creatures.

Developing the Naturalistic Intelligence

After asking your students about holding sand and water, the unit proceeds to query them about holding three animals. Those children who are familiar with animals will have some definite ideas about holding

cats, raccoons, and bears. You might ask your students which of the pairs of animals would be easiest to hold (assuming that the bears are small cubs).

Developing the Visual-Spatial Intelligence

Space is given at the end of the unit for the student to show (in pencil or some other medium) how the bears can be held. Give as much time for this task as your students need to try to draw or otherwise represent their solution to the problem. This is the kind of task that allows the youngsters with superior visual-spatial skills to excel.

Developing the Mathematical-Logical Intelligence

The last series of questions about holding bears begs the question of the *size* of the bears. The logical thinker will quickly ask this question before attempting to try to answer questions about holding one or two bears in his arms.

Following Through

In Your Hands opens up a variety of topics that can be followed up:

* Do people try to hold water in their hands? Why and in what situations?
* When was the last time you held sand in your hands—at the beach or in a sandbox? What are the usual ways for carrying sand when people need to use it or move it? When did people first start using tools for transporting sand and dirt?
* What about trying to handle wild animals—is it usually safe? (Generally, baby animals don't pose too much of a problem, but it depends on the species and the individual animals.)

In Your Hands

Can you hold water in your hands? _____ How much water can you hold in your hands?

_____

_____

Can you hold sand in your hands? _____ How much sand can you hold in your hands?

_____

Can you hold a cat in your hands? _____

_____

Can you hold two cats in your arms? _____ Are you sure?

_____

Can you hold a bear in your arms? _____ Why or why not?

_____

_____

Can you hold two bears in your arms? _____ Why or why not?

_____

_____

If you can, show how you can hold two bears in your arms (on the back of this piece of paper).

Unit 40

Riding a Sunbeam

Setting the Stage for the Unit

This is a fanciful unit. It is not based on keen observation, but on sensitivity and imagination. The fantasy proposed is that the children are to imagine themselves as being very, very small—small enough to ride on a sunbeam. It may be that one or more of the children have actually had this fantasy. One of the blessings of childhood is that such fantasies are permissible. When your students are older, daydreams won't be considered appropriate, especially in school. You can lead into the unit by making a remark or two about the sun's rays, or sunbeams. They are prominently featured in many famous paintings, and you just might have one available to show your students how lovely and important sunbeams are.

Administering the Unit

The following activities can accompany the administration of Riding a Sunbeam:

Developing the Naturalistic Intelligence

The sunbeam, as we see it inside or outside, is a phenomenon that occurs often (on sunny days), but is just uncommon enough to grab our attention. When rays of light slant down from a cloud, they are especially impressive. Ask your students if they have seen this kind of sunbeam. The kind they may think of is the ray of light that comes through a window into a room. You can ask your students why we don't see the sun's rays all of the time, even when the sun is shining.

Developing the Visual-Spatial Intelligence

At the end of the unit, your students are invited to depict themselves riding a sunbeam. Before they begin, ask them if the sunbeam is taking them anywhere in particular. Some children may have no destination in mind, whereas others will think of wonderful places to escape to. Allow them to choose any medium they would like for their depiction—pencil, pastels, watercolor, marking pens, crayon, and so on.

Following Through

One of E. Paul Torrance's creative thinking skills is "enjoying and using fantasy." When fantasy is considered legitimate, Torrance believes, the individual feels free to consider all kinds of possibilities and relationships. With this unit you can make fantastic thinking legitimate by having your students extend their comments about riding a sunbeam and their pictures of doing so by writing stories of what would happen were such an event to take place.

Riding a Sunbeam

Does the sun shining through a window remind you of a magic slide? What other things does a sunbeam remind you of?

_____

_____

_____

_____

If you were very, very small, you could ride on a sunbeam. How would it feel to ride on a sunbeam?

_____

_____

_____

_____

What would happen if you were to ride a sunbeam? Where would you go? Draw a picture of your sunny ride.

Unit 41

Just Dreaming

Setting the Stage for the Unit

This unit focuses on the simple task of drawing a ladybug beetle and two other insects. The drawing requires a little skill, however, since it is supposed to represent the moment in a dream that the student—who has become a ladybug—confronts an ant tending her aphid. You can lead into the unit by asking your students if they have ever dreamed that they were an animal or an insect.

Administering the Unit

The following are activities that can accompany the administration of Just Dreaming:

Developing the Naturalistic Intelligence

The scene the student is supposed to draw most certainly is a common one in spring and summer. Ants are zealous caretakers of aphids, getting honeydew from them in much the same way that a dairy farmer gets milk from cows, and aphids constitute a chief source of food for ladybugs. A confrontation between an ant and a ladybug over an aphid raises some interesting questions. Which insect wins? Does the ant, with its mandibles and formic acid, usually drive off any ladybug who attempts to eat an aphid? The naturalists in your class may have some ideas about this

little drama. Ask your students if they have ever been bitten by an ant. Some species of ant can give a particularly painful bite. It won't be possible for your students to draw the ant, aphid, and ladybug without doing a little research concerning the appearance and behavior of these insects.

Developing the Verbal-Linguistic Intelligence

Your students are likely to become intrigued by the question of what happens when a ladybug approaches an aphid being tended to by an ant. Your students will probably want to comment about the situation before drawing, but don't let them just speculate. Have them read about the insects and then report what they have learned.

Following Through

If this activity is successful, you might pose similar problems concerning insects and other animals:

* What happens when a butterfly and a bee land on the same flower?
* What happens when a single crow encounters an owl just after dusk?
* What happens when a prairie dog enters its burrow and discovers it is occupied by a snake?

Just Dreaming

Let's say you dream that you are a ladybug beetle. In your dream you are in a vegetable garden. It is summer, and you are busy looking for something to eat. You have flown to a bean plant and are approaching several aphids when you are confronted by an ant that is "tending" the aphids.

Draw a picture of yourself, as the ladybug, with the aphids, and the ant. Put in all of the details of such a scene. You may have to consult several books about insects.

The next night you dream you are an ant, but as an ant you dream that you are a human. Imagine what kind of human you, as an ant, dream that you are. Then draw a picture of what you think an ant would dream a human would be doing—that is, if an ant could dream.

Unit 42

Your Favorite Things

Setting the Stage for the Unit

In contrast with some of the units in this book, Your Favorite Things is entirely serious. Accordingly, your students should be in a fairly reflective mood when you administer it to them. After a "free reading" period is an ideal time. You might ask a question or two about how your students acquire their preferences. It's a good bet that most of them have never given any thought to just how they came to prefer chocolate over vanilla and strawberry, or red over blue and green. Their answers may surprise you—and them!

Administering the Unit

Following are a few of the ways you can use "Your Favorite Things" to encourage the development of multiple intelligences in your students:

Developing the Intrapersonal Intelligence

This unit should be administered to the children individually. In general, their responses are not meant to be shared with their classmates.

Some of the questions asked of your students in this unit are not the usual ones that are asked on personal inventory instruments. For example, after asking them what living thing they like most, you ask whether they will always like it so much. The students can't know, of course, but the question will cause them to reflect a little about their current preferences.

Developing the Verbal-Linguistic Intelligence

There are quite a few questions to answer in this unit, and we hope your students will attempt to answer all of them. Students who are good at expressing their feelings will be able to communicate their ideas accurately.

Developing the Interpersonal Intelligence

The last question—about whether it is better to love people and animals as opposed to things—is perhaps too philosophical for young children. Nevertheless, it is an important question for children growing up. Some love their dolls and toys inordinately, but not unnaturally. The impermanence of toys and the mortality of living things are considerations that children have to face at some time, and each of your students has probably done so because of the loss of a pet or the loss or breaking of a toy. Those youngsters who have a high degree of interpersonal intelligence will recognize the significance of the question.

Developing the Naturalistic Intelligence

Animals and plants are very important to children who love nature, and so they would be expected to favor living things when responding to the final question. Some adults prefer their pets to any other living things, and perhaps you have students who have the same high regard for a pet; but your students aren't asked to decide whether they prefer animals to people in this unit.

Following Through

If you enjoy reading to your class, you might follow up this unit by reading one of James Herriot's stories about his clients' devotion to their pets. Of the many suitable ones are "Humphrey" in *James Herriot's Dog Stories* and "The Christmas Day Kitten" in *James Herriot's Treasury for Children*, which deals with the mortality of animals. There are countless other excellent stories about pets and their owners, but Herriot has a masterful way of portraying both the pet and its adoring owner.

Your Favorite Things

Each of us has things that mean a lot to us. You must have a toy that you like more than any other toy you have. And there probably is a program on television that you try not to miss. Have you thought about the things in your life that you like very, very much?

What do you like most that is alive? _____

Why do you like that living thing so much?

_____

_____

_____

_____

Will you like the living thing as much next month as you do now?

_____ Why or why not?

_____

_____

_____

_____

Learning from Nature © 2005 • www.zephyrpress.com

Will you always like the living thing as much as you do now?
_____ If so, how can you be sure?

_____

_____

_____

_____

What is your favorite thing that is not alive? _____ Why
do you like it?

_____

_____

_____

_____

Is it better to love people and animals or things that are not alive?
_____ Why do you think so?

_____

_____

_____

_____

Unit 43

Mixing

Setting the Stage for the Unit

This unit will probably be most successful if it follows Seasons (Unit 48), since it deals principally with the times of the year when it's best to undertake certain activities.

Mixing asks a number of questions—some easy and some quite difficult—which means that your students will tend to sail through some and hesitate with others. The ideal way of introducing the lesson is to mix something in front of the class. It can be anything readily available that the children are familiar with, such as detergent and water (for dishwashing), tempera powder and water (for painting), lemons, water, and sugar (for lemonade), and dirt and water (to make mud pies).

Another way of warming up your students is to ask a question or two, such as "Do you think I'd enjoy myself if I went looking for wildflowers today?" (when it is winter) or "Do you think I'd enjoy going for a hike today?" (when it is raining or snowing).

Administering the Unit

The following activities can accompany the administration of Mixing:

Developing the Naturalistic and Visual-Spatial Intelligences

Your students may be challenged when it comes to drawing a snowstorm or a thunderstorm. Does the thunderstorm affect the trees? Is it accompanied by rain, wind, or visible lightning? Is a picture of a snowstorm, as the joke would have it, just a piece of blank white paper? Those students who are sensitive to changes in the weather will have some ideas. The picture of the snowstorm can show drifts, tops of snow-laden trees bending, people defending themselves, cars stalled by the side of the road, and many other indicators.

Developing the Verbal-Linguistic Intelligence

If your students seem puzzled by the questions of the unit, one or more may enjoy doing some research about storms (a number of television programs have been devoted to hurricanes and other storms). One of the students might even give an oral presentation about the creation of a thunderstorm, a tornado, a hurricane or of weather patterns, possibly with visuals to make the processes clearer.

Developing the Intrapersonal Intelligence

The final section of the unit asks the students to say what they would mix together to get a good day, a bad day, good music, a smile, a good grade, and a good feeling at home. These questions bring out the sensitivities of your students and may provide insights about them.

Following Through

Since we mix everything from people (when people gather for social "mixers") to chemicals (in laboratories), you will have a wide range of topics to explore if you wish to follow up this unit with a similar activity. A pharmacist does a great deal of mixing, and you might invite one to class to talk about what he or she does. The children might also explore some of the processes in nature in which combining elements creates new materials. For example, you could have them research an oxide that they are familiar with, such as dry ice (solidified carbon dioxide) or rubies (aluminum oxide).

Unit 43

Mixing

If a movement of air is mixed with water, fog, hail, or rain can form. It all depends on how they mix. And when a slightly different movement of air is mixed with water, we get snow. In fact, machines can now make snow. Why would anyone want to *make* snow?

_____

_____

_____

If the air moves very fast, there can be a storm. It can be a thunderstorm. Draw a thunderstorm in the city.

Or it can be a snowstorm. Draw a snowstorm in the country.

Is air ever totally still? _____
Nature mixes air and water and gives us fog, rain, and snow. You can mix things, too.

If you mix water and salt, what will you get?

_____

If you mix milk and chocolate, what will you get?

_____

If you mix flour and water, what will you get?

_____

What can you do with it?

_____

What would you mix together to get

a good day? _____

a bad day? _____

good music? _____

a smile? _____

a good grade? _____

a good feeling at home? _____

Fly, Fly

Setting the Stage for the Unit

This unit is partly about fantasy and partly about reality, but mostly we would like your students to be imaginative. To get them in the mood to be fanciful, you can lead in with some comments about birds or show a model of an airplane or a photograph of a bird such as a gull or hawk soaring–anything to get your students to think about flying.

Administering the Unit

A few ideas about how Fly, Fly can be administered to encourage your students to develop their multiple intelligences follow:

Developing the Verbal-Linguistic Intelligence

The primary objective of this unit is to get your students to write. We hope that they do get in a "flying" state of mind. A film or video to portray flight might help, but we want the young people to use their imaginations when they respond to the questions about how they might fly. You could ask them to think of words that describe birds. As they come up with them, you could write them on the chalkboard. This should give them a vocabulary source and some stimulation for their writing.

Developing the Bodily-Kinesthetic Intelligence

Before asking your students to write about their flying, we invite them to show how they would fly. Birds flap, dive, soar, flutter, glide, dart, dip and wheel, and swoop, and you can assume there will be some differences in the demonstrations.

Developing the Naturalistic Intelligence

This unit provides another opportunity for the child who is fascinated by animals, and especially birds, to share his or her knowledge. The student may point out that there is a tremendous difference in the various species of birds, and perhaps that a few birds can't fly at all (ostrich, rhea, penguin, emu, and cassowary).

Developing the Intrapersonal Intelligence

The students are invited to imagine that they can fly and to envision just how they will fly. It has always been a natural desire of people to want to fly, and children are certainly no exception. Peter Pan is such a popular character, in part, for that reason.

Following Through

For follow-up activities for Fly, Fly, consider asking the students to investigate the physics of flight, and to do some research about how animals—or humankind—first came to fly. If one of your students has a relative who works in the aircraft/airline industry, a field trip could be arranged.

Fly, Fly

Have you ever wanted to fly? In a well-known story, Peter Pan was able to fly. How did he fly? Did he fly like a bee? Did he fly like a pigeon? Did he fly like a parrot?

If you could fly, would you fly very high? _____ Why or why not?

_____

_____

Would you fly very fast? _____ Why or why not?

_____

_____

Would you fly all of the time? _____ Why or why not?

_____

_____

Would you want anyone else to be able to fly, too? _____
Whom would you want to be able to fly?

_____

Would you rather fly like a helicopter or like a robin?
_____ Why?

_____

Is there anything that flies like a helicopter? _____

What is it? _____
Would you ever get tired of flying? _____ Why or why not?

_____

Would you want to walk sometimes? _____ Why or why not?

_____

Show how you would fly.

Tell what would happen.

_____

_____

_____

Unit 45

Sing While You Work

Setting the Stage for the Unit

Some people, including seven famous little men, whistle while they work, but we are not suggesting to your students that they always sing or hum as they work. We are aware that such behavior in the classroom would seem unusual, if not downright improper. In Sing While You Work, we do encourage your students to sing or hum while they work on this unit.

To put your students in the mood for the unit, play a recording of something tuneful. It might be best to have the volume low and to choose a pleasant vocal rendition. The music shouldn't be too obvious or distracting. The timing of administering the unit is important. Choose a time when the children aren't antsy.

Administering the Unit

A few activities that encourage your students to develop their multiple intelligences and work well with Sing While You Work are:

Developing the Musical-Rhythmical Intelligence

This unit isn't just for the musically talented; all of your students can hum and will enjoy the experience. We've known primary teachers who didn't mind some humming when their students worked, but you may prefer to restrict the activity to only this one time.

Developing the Visual-Spatial Intelligence

We ask your students to draw a picture of an animal singing or humming while working. It could be a bird, of course, but it also could be a bee. At any rate, the student is humming while working at a drawing of an animal humming or singing while it works. This part of the unit will appeal to the imaginative and artistically talented child.

Developing the Verbal-Linguistic Intelligence

In addition to the drawing task, this unit asks for quite a bit of writing. Some children won't respond very fully to the prompts, so we urge you to encourage your students to answer the questions in full. Those who enjoy writing will try to express their ideas in effective and colorful ways.

Developing the Naturalistic Intelligence

Aside from the musical aspect of the unit, there is the subject of animals singing and humming. Before your students begin to make their sketches, you might ask the class to have a discussion about which animals hum or sing. If someone complains during this discussion that a bee is not an animal, the youngster who is a student of nature will probably comment that insects are indeed animals. Such an exchange could be used as a lead-in to a discussion of the taxonomy of living things.

Following Through

If there is a discussion of how scientists classify living things, you will have an opportunity to introduce your students to this branch of the life sciences.

Your students may also want to look further into the matter of the sounds that animals make. There is a tremendous variety of them, and they are fascinating. Lions, coyotes, wolves, crickets, cicadas, whales, frogs, mules, ostriches (which can grunt like lions), and most other animals make noises for many reasons. It's probably unnecessary to have the children research the logic of the various animal sounds; if they make a serious effort to mimic, or sing, the animal sounds, they will have enough to inquire about. Some of the students may have heard the recordings of whales "singing." The question of what exactly qualifies as singing could lead to additional learning.

Sing While You Work

Have you seen someone singing while working? _____
Who was it?

_____

Was it your mother or father working at home? _____

Does it help to sing while you are working? _____
Why or why not?

_____

_____

Could it help if you were able to sing or hum or whistle while you are working at school?

_____

When would it be all right?

_____

When would it not be all right?

_____

Are there any animals that sing or hum while they are working?

_____

Draw a picture of one. Sing or hum while you are drawing the picture. (Ask your teacher first if you are at school.)

Did you sing or hum while you were drawing? _____

Did it help you to draw better? _____

Three

Setting the Stage for the Unit

This is the kind of unit that takes time to develop. You may want to try it when your schedule is not crowded. It involves both reflective thinking and bodily activity, so you might think about where the children can move about as well as where they can settle quietly and ponder.

If, unfortunately, a fly is an unwelcome visitor to your classroom, referring to it may serve as a good lead-in to Three. Flies aren't very often the subject of much conjecture in the classroom, but in this case the insects occupy a prominent place.

Administering the Unit

Following are some ways of using Three to encourage the development of multiple intelligences in your students:

Developing the Bodily-Kinesthetic Intelligence

This unit invites your students to do a good deal of moving when imitating the characteristic movements of the turtle, firefighter, and fly. We hope that a space can be designated for acting out the movements. Although all of your students are familiar with how flies move, some research about the various turtles that are found in North America may be necessary before "Mr. Turtle" can be imitated. For instance, how do sea turtles swim? How the firefighter's movements are pantomimed should prove interesting.

Developing the Naturalistic Intelligence

Three should appeal to the student who is a keen observer of people, animals, and plants. It asks questions that are rarely, if ever, asked, such as "Can you imagine when you might see a turtle, a fly, and a fire-fighter all at once?" To come up with an answer, the student must invent a scenario that culminates in the three coming into close proximity. The student who is very interested in nature will probably volunteer that a fly is an insect and a turtle is a reptile.

Developing the Interpersonal Intelligence

If it seems advisable, the class can be divided into groups of three for the purpose of pantomiming the three characters in the unit. More information about turtles, firefighters, and flies will probably be needed. Books at the reading levels of your students have been written about turtles and firefighters—we haven't seen any with flies as the main subject—and should be available in your school library or a public library. A good deal has been written about firefighters and their heroic deeds on September 11, 2001, at the World Trade Center in New York. Your students should have access to that information also.

Developing the Verbal-Linguistic Intelligence

Even though you might see some head-scratching, you should let your students know that you expect them to respond to the questions in the unit. The students who are good writers should be able to adequately express their ideas about the turtle, fire-fighter, and fly. At the end of the unit, they will be challenged to explain why there are animals such as flies. The existence of a creature like the turtle isn't often questioned, but people have been looking for a reason for the fly's existence for a very long time.

Developing the Intrapersonal Intelligence

The unit opens with queries about how the student feels about a turtle, a firefighter, and a fly. Our intent is to have the students probe their emotions and attitudes about each of the three. The thoughtful child will have some interesting reflections concerning the highly diverse animals.

Following Through

You can see that variations of this exercise might be devised to help your students acquire a tremendous range of information and gain a deeper understanding of objects, events, and processes that are presented to their senses. We recommend that you try this exercise again as a follow-up and note any changes in your students' abilities to see relationships and to communicate the insights they receive. You might pick three other things—say, a tiger, a musician playing an instrument, and an outboard motor—and have the students interpret the sound each makes. It might become a bit noisy, but if the children are serious about making accurate interpretations, there will be no complaints from down the hall.

Three

This is a turtle. What do you think about when you see a turtle?

_____

_____

Here is a firefighter at his fire station. What do you think about when you see a firefighter?

_____

_____

The insect you see here is a fly. When you see a fly, what do you think about?

_____

_____

Can you imagine a time when you see a turtle, a firefighter, and a fly all at once?

_____

_____

How do turtles move in the water?

_____

How do firefighters move when they are going to a fire?

_____

How do flies move on a hot day in the summer?

_____

Why don't you show how a turtle, a firefighter, and a fly move? If you would like to, you can also write some words that tell about each one.

Mr. Turtle

_____

_____

Mr. Firefighter

_____

_____

Mr. Fly

_____

_____

_____

Why are there such things as flies and turtles?

_____

_____

_____

_____

_____

_____

_____

Have you had any other ideas about animals and how they live?

_____

_____

_____

_____

_____

_____

_____

Four

Setting the Stage for the Unit

Four is essentially an exercise in relating dissimilar phenomena, that is, in abstracting. It is the kind of exercise that, for most classes, takes some leading into. A good way of preparing your students for the unit is to pick up two or three objects that are on or near your desk. They could be, for example, a compass, a chalkboard eraser, and a calendar. You could ask your class, "In what ways are these items different?" (The range of responses could be impressive.) Then you might ask, "How are the three objects alike?" There are many ways of looking for likenesses in objects. Here are some approaches your students may take:

* Are they animate or inanimate? (Are they alive?)
* Are they all manufactured? Do they occur naturally in their present form?
* Are they made of the same kind of material?
* Are they usually used by the same person?
* Are they made for the same general purpose?
* Are they found in the same general area?
* Are they self-propelled, or do they need something to make them function?
* Were they invented in the twentieth century?
* Do they all make noises? Do they make the same kind of noise?
* Are they the same color?
* Do they all have an odor?
* Do they all conduct electricity?
* Do they all have something to do with writing?
* Are they flexible? (Do they all bend?)
* Do they all oxidize? (Do they all rust?)
* Do they all conduct heat fairly well?

If an affirmative answer can be given to any of these questions, the student has made an abstraction.

Administering the Unit

Following are only a few ways in which Four can be used to encourage the development of multiple intelligences:

Developing the Logical-Mathematical Intelligence

In addition to reacting to the questions about a squirrel, a woman musician, a male carpenter, and a rainbow, your students are asked to compare them. How are they alike? These abstractions are at the heart of the unit. This activity allows the child who naturally sees connections and commonalities to shine.

Developing the Intrapersonal Intelligence

The unit begins by asking your students to record what they think of when they see a squirrel, a woman making music, a man hammering a nail, and a rainbow. The only way for a student to make the associations naturally is to do it alone. If you ask for reactions from the class at large, many students will be unable to record their associations spontaneously. It will be up to you to decide if the children should share their impressions and insights once they have all finished. In any event, we recommend that each student mentally chew the material in Four on his or her own before becoming engaged in a group discussion.

Developing the Verbal-Linguistic Intelligence

The responses called for are on the order of impressions, and for that reason, your students are not expected to pay too much attention to spelling, grammar, and punctuation. They should be encouraged to express themselves clearly, however, and to write legibly. Their ideas are what matter. The unit also offers an opportunity for students to enrich their vocabularies (rodent, saxophone, carpenter, prism, etc.).

Developing the Naturalistic Intelligence

Two of the four items are "from" nature, and students who are inclined to watch wildlife or to consider the conditions that produce a rainbow can be encouraged to think more deeply about those phenomena and investigate them. The sounds emanating from a squirrel, a man hammering a nail, and a saxophone differ widely, and the youngster who is interested in sound can find out more about how they are produced. "How do you tell the difference between a saxophone and a trumpet?" you might ask.

Developing the Bodily-Kinesthetic Intelligence

Although your students aren't asked to do more than name games that feature four players, they can be encouraged to demonstrate those games that may not be known to everyone in the class.

Developing the Musical-Rhythmical Intelligence

You can play a recording of a saxophone to illustrate its characteristic sounds. If the music is jazz, you might encourage your students to respond by clapping or even singing.

Developing the Visual-Spatial Intelligence

For those who enjoy drawing and need opportunities to demonstrate their talent, you can suggest that they make a picture of one or more of their impressions of the four subjects.

Following Through

You may wish to present other exercises that will give your students practice in seeing relationships of this kind. If so, there are at least three ways to present exercises comparable to Four. You can give your students three or four pictures (photographs or illustrations) to compare for likenesses. You can present the exercises verbally, giving only words (either spoken or written) for the items. Or you can present the items with both words and pictures. Each of these techniques has its advantages. For younger children, illustrations are often necessary to make the concept clear and to trigger their imaginations. On the other hand, illustrations may interfere somewhat with the abstraction process for older students by giving them dominant images that tend to obscure other images.

An alternate exercise would be to reverse the procedure by giving the students some quality or trait and having them think of four or more things that possess this quality. In fact, they might like to write poems in the style of Mary O'Neill's *Hailstones and Halibut Bones* (Doubleday, 1961). Instead of writing on color, as Mary O'Neill did, they might like to write on numbers, days of the week, etc.

Four

What do you think of when you see

. . . a squirrel?

_____

_____

. . . a woman making music?

_____

_____

. . . a man hammering a nail?

_____

_____

. . . a rainbow?

_____

_____

How are the squirrel, the woman making music, the man hammering a nail, and the rainbow different?

_____

_____

_____

_____

_____

_____

Are they alike in any way? _____ If they are alike in any way, tell in what way they are alike.

_____

_____

_____

_____

_____

Unit 48

Seasons

Setting the Stage for the Unit

No matter how old we grow, the changing of seasons never fails to fascinate us. It is the same for children, but it is newer to them. All the same, they take the rhythms of seasonal change for granted. The onset of winter comes slowly in many places, tempered and presaged by the slow and colorful disintegration of nature in the fall. Children are sensitive to seasonal changes, and they certainly are made aware of them in classrooms whose decorations, exhibits, and even the curriculum herald the new season. You might introduce the topic of seasons by asking your students to name their favorite season.

Administering the Unit

Among the many ways of using Seasons to encourage your students to develop their multiple intelligences are the following:

Developing the Naturalistic Intelligence

This unit is designed to provoke several emotions as well as some wondering and seeking. For example, there are places where people only experience one season, and we ask where they might be. One place is Guatemala, where they have "eternal spring." Your students can ask questions about that remarkable situation and then learn about such places. At the end of the unit, your students are asked if there are seasons in the ocean. Although this question may be somewhat advanced for your class, your students can try to find out the answer (which is yes).

Developing the Visual-Spatial Intelligence

If the colors of autumn or spring especially appeal to your students, they can draw a favorite scene of that season. It might be that they prefer a winter scene, perhaps of ice skating or sledding.

Developing the Verbal-Linguistic Intelligence

Seasons invites your students to write about places where there is only one season and about seasons in the oceans of the world—not particularly easy subjects to write about. They aren't asked to describe their feelings about the seasons, but to look into situations they know little or nothing about. Accordingly, your students may need some guidance from you about where to get answers to these questions.

Developing the Interpersonal Intelligence

This activity is a search for information. If there is enough interest, the class can be broken up into groups of four or five in order to acquire the information needed to answer either or both of the questions posed in the unit. The various members of the groups could be assigned to find the information from different sourceson the Internet, from reference books and periodicals at their reading level, by asking authorities, or by consulting maps of the world's climate and topography.

Following Through

Following the completion of this unit, you can cover other topics relating to the seasons. For example, your students can do the planning for and decorating of a bulletin board featuring winter, spring, or summer. Or they could compose verses about the seasons after you have read some well-known seasonal poems to them, such as "Spring is showery, flowery, bowering" (Mother Goose), Amy Lowell's "The City of Falling Leaves," Robert Louis Stevenson's "Autumn Fires," or Dorothy Aldis's "Ice." You might also have your students put on a skit or a play about a season.

Seasons

Where we live, in the spring the days get longer and warmer. Trees sprout leaves, and the grass grows fast. Insects and animals are born.

In the summer, plants grow taller, and fruits and vegetables get bigger. Animals have lots of food to eat.

In the fall, many trees begin to lose their leaves. There is still a lot of food for animals to eat. Some birds and animals leave and go to where it is warmer.

In the winter, many plants and insects die. Some animals have very little to eat. Many trees have no leaves.

And when spring comes again, the same things happen all over again. There is a beginning, a time of growth, and an ending to most living things on earth. For many plants and insects, their beginning, growth, and ending lasts only one year. For many plants, the beginning, growth, and ending will happen again and again for many years.

In some places on earth, there is only one season. Where are those places? What happens to the plants and animals there? Find out what happens in those places and tell about it.

_____

_____

_____

_____

_____

_____

_____

_____

_____

Are there seasons in the ocean? _____ Find out if the ocean has seasons. Tell what you find out.

_____

_____

_____

_____

_____

_____

_____

_____

Unit 49

What Is the Best Time?

Setting the Stage for the Unit

This unit will probably be most successful if it follows Seasons, since it deals principally with the times of the year when it is best to undertake certain activities. In order to warm up your students, you might ask a question or two, such as: "Do you think I'd enjoy myself if I went out looking for wildflowers today?" (when it is winter) or "Do you think I'd enjoy going for a hike today?" (when it is snowing or raining).

Administering the Unit

Most of the questions on the handout relate to nature, but two do not. One of the exceptions asks which season is best for visiting a sick person. The ideal response to the question might be, "Anytime!" Or an answer that is perhaps even better could be, "When the sick person needs a visitor." At any rate, visiting sick people isn't a seasonal pastime. The responses to the "Whys" should be especially significant.
A few activities that can be used with What Is the Best Time? are:

Developing the Naturalistic and Verbal-Linguistic Intelligences

After your students respond to the questions, it would be instructive to have them evaluate one another's responses—but not harshly. For example, a child might want to go for a hike when the weather is blustery. That's when many people find nature interesting and exciting. To dismiss such a choice would be doing an injustice to that individual.

Developing the Visual-Spatial Intelligence

A natural activity that can grow out of this unit is to have the children depict one of the scenes in pencil, crayon, watercolor, pastel, or ink.

Developing the Bodily-Kinesthetic Intelligence

The children might enjoy pantomiming the activities and having their classmates guess what they are.

Following Through

An obvious follow-up question for your students is to ask them to describe their "best time." If they are capable of expressing their ideas in writing, it would allow all of them to relate a favorite occasion. Certain students, as you know, tend to dominate a general discussion, and the shy student often doesn't get to contribute.

What Is the Best Time?

Some times are better than other times to do certain things. For example, swimming in a river is more fun and safer in the summer than in the winter. Most of us prefer to read books when the weather is rainy or snowy.

We have four seasons—winter, spring, summer, and fall. What is the best season to

...go on a picnic? _____ Why is that a good time?

_____

...rake leaves? _____ Why is that a good time?

_____

...pick berries? _____ Why is that a good time?

_____

...take a hike? _____ Why is that a good time?

_____

...watch a football game? _____ Why is that a good time?

_____

...ride a bike? _____ Why is that a good time?

_____

...visit a sick person? _____ Why is that a good time?

_____

...watch fireflies? _____ Why is that a good time?

_____

. . . see a robin? _____ Why is that a good time?

_____

. . . go sledding? _____ Why is that a good time?

_____

. . . build a fort? _____ Why is that a good time?

_____

. . . fly a kite? _____ Why is that a good time?

_____

Unit 50

Afraid?

Setting the Stage for the Unit

This unit touches on a matter that can be serious; that is, the irrational fears people have of some animals. Are these fears instinctual or inherited? There is a great deal of debate as to whether the fear of snakes, for example, is an instinctive reaction that is part of our being human. Setting aside that particular debate, it seems probable that children acquire most of their fears through direct experience or indirectly from their parents and other adults. The unit deliberately starts with three silly questions about the emotions that three quite different animals trigger. We suggest that you lead into the unit and those three questions by asking a similar question, something along the lines of either "Do ladybugs make you scared?" or "Do flies make you giggle?"

Administering the Unit

The following are activities that can accompany this unit:

Developing the Naturalistic Intelligence

Most (but not all) professional naturalists are unafraid of the living things that they study. As stated in the unit, however, there are biologists who are afraid of snakes, or so they say. The budding naturalists in your class are not likely to be fearful of too many creatures. They are interested in the creatures, not intimidated by them. Most of your class, however, is probably afraid of animals such as bats, either because of their appearance or what has been said about them. A discussion of bats or snakes will help allay these fears, as would a classroom visit from a person who keeps or trains these animals—especially if he or she brought the animals along.

Developing the Verbal-Linguistic Intelligence

A student might want to present an oral report about any of the animals mentioned in the unit. This activity should be voluntary.

Developing the Visual-Spatial Intelligence

Similarly, if a child is fascinated by an animal mentioned in the unit, she or he can draw or even paint a likeness of it.

Following Through

The subject of this unit is fear of animals. It is one of the most important subjects in this book, and we leave it up to you as to how you administer the unit and follow through with it. The fears of childhood can be alleviated, if not eliminated, by discussions with peers and adults. For so many people to be afraid of spiders—especially since the average person so rarely encounters a poisonous one—is most surprising. You might mention some of the animals that people are commonly afraid of, such as mice and spiders, and then encourage your students to talk about why these animals are so terrifying to some people.

Afraid?

Do spiders make you laugh? Do monkeys make you cry? Do sparrows make you feel angry?

Probably not. But animals do affect people by just being themselves. The sight of a snake can frighten even a scientist who is trained to observe animals. When someone has an unreasonable fear, it is called a phobia. Many people have phobias about snakes, spiders, and even cats—although they have never been harmed directly by these animals.

How are you affected by these animals? What kind of feeling do you have when you see them?

Grizzly bear _____

Trout _____

Mongoose _____

Tiger _____

Dragonfly _____

Box turtle _____

Koala _____

Rattlesnake _____

Walrus _____

Moth _____

Shark _____

Squirrel _____

Tarantula _____

Vulture _____

Penguin _____

Rat _____

Moray eel _____

Porpoise _____

Bat _____

Cockroach _____

Who or what might be frightened by a flying squirrel?

_____

Where and when might it happen?

_____

_____

_____

Who or what might be afraid of a robin? _____

When and where might it happen?

_____

_____

_____

What Comes Next?

Setting the Stage for the Unit

This unit is all about sequence, or seeing the natural order of things. There are 10 questions concerning what follows what. Altogether that makes quite a few, so you might want to administer the unit in two parts. To get started, you can pick any number of natural events and ask questions about them. Two possibilities are "What follows lightning?" and "What comes after a freeze?"

Administering the Unit

The following activities can accompany the administration of What Comes Next?:

Developing the Naturalistic Intelligence

One or two of the questions are a bit tricky. The answer to "What follows an airplane?" could be "A jet trail" if the student is thinking of big commercial planes, but many planes do not have jet engines. "What follows a grasshopper?" can be answered in several ways. If you live in a rural area, the answers could be "Crop failure" or "Birds."

Developing the Visual-Spatial Intelligence

Any of the scenes suggested by the questions might be depicted in drawings. Some of the scenes could be humorous, such as those created in response to the question "What follows a mop?"

Developing the Verbal-Linguistic Intelligence

Several of the questions are worthy of a serious class discussion. For example, the question about the elephant might merit discussion. Elephants do a great deal of damage to trees when they are crowded into a confined area. Although we generally view them as huge but benign animals, elephants can be devastating to plant growth.

Following Through

You can ask your students any other "What follows . . ." questions that are pertinent to your curriculum. For example, in the area of language arts these questions are fundamental:

* What follows a question? (question mark)
* What follows an expression of strong feeling? (an exclamation mark)
* What follows a period? (usually a new sentence)
* What follows a salutation in a letter? ("Dear _____") (a comma or a colon)
* What follows "Sincerely" in a business letter? (a signature)

What Comes Next?

What follows a mouse? _____ Why?

_____

_____

What follows a duck? _____ Why?

_____

_____

What follows night? _____ Why?

_____

_____

What follows an airplane? _____ Why?

_____

_____

AN, HY ✳

9 What follows nine? _____ Why?

_____

_____

_____

What follows a grasshopper? _____ Why?

_____

_____

What follows snow? _____ Why?

_____

_____

What follows a mop? _____ Why?

_____

_____

_____

Thank You — What follows "Thank you"? _____ Why?

_____

_____

What follows sleep? _____ Why?

_____

_____

_____

Learning from Nature © 2005 • www.zephyrpress.com

Where Have You Seen This Before?

Setting the Stage for the Unit

Where Have You Seen This Before? is concerned with waste. Accordingly, you can lead into the unit when there are instances of waste in your classroom or when there is senseless waste in the community. The examples given in the unit are common enough, but there are innumerable occasions when people waste resources. Conserving water, electricity, and gasoline are in the news when there is a shortage of one or more of them, but people tend to forget about conserving when supplies increase and prices go down. Children can remind adults about conserving precious resources and do a great deal about it themselves.

Administering the Unit

Following are activities that you can administer in conjunction with the unit in order to provide opportunities for students to develop their intelligences:

Developing the Visual-Spatial Intelligence

At the end of the unit, your students are invited to draw a scene of one or more individuals wasting something. Those students who enjoy expressing themselves through drawing will be able to convey their ideas more fully by using a pencil, crayon, chalk, or pen.

Developing the Verbal-Linguistic Intelligence

Throughout the unit your students are asked to express their ideas in writing, but Where Have You Seen This Before? can also be administered orally so that children who are adept at expressing themselves in discussions can use that talent. You may wish to have your students write a quasi-essay about waste in their community. Such essays occasionally get published in local newspapers. The children can also devise slogans for fighting waste and conserving resources.

Developing the Bodily-Kinesthetic Intelligence

To reinforce the ideas about wasting or conserving resources, you could have the children make up and put on a skit illustrating the wasting or conserving of a resource that means something to them.

Developing the Interpersonal Intelligence

Allow the youngsters to conceptualize, plan, organize, and perform their skit. Those students who have ideas and those who are good at working with others will have opportunities to develop their abilities.

Developing the Naturalistic Intelligence

The children who feel most keenly about preserving nature and preventing damage to it will probably take the lead in any discussion about wasting trees; polluting lakes, rivers, and oceans; despoiling the countryside; or, on the positive side, preserving a natural resource.

Following Through

At the conclusion of the unit, your students can do some investigating in the school and in the community to find out if food, water, electricity, paper, gasoline, and other resources are being wasted. If they find situations where the resources are being wasted and there is something they can do about it, encourage them to take appropriate actions.

Where Have You Seen This Before?

Have you seen this happen recently?

_____

If so, when did it happen?

_____

_____

Where did it happen?

_____

_____

_____

Have you seen something like this lately?

_____

If so, when did you see it?

_____

_____

Where did you see it?

_____

_____

Have you seen this happen recently?

_____

If so, when did it happen?

_____

_____

Where did it happen?

_____

_____

_____

How are the three scenes similar?

_____

_____

_____

Can you think of a scene that is like the three scenes but is a different situation? Describe it.

_____

_____

_____

If you'd like to draw a picture of the scene, here is some space for the illustration.

Unit 53

For a Better World

Setting the Stage for the Unit

This is a "just suppose" kind of unit, and you would, ideally, give it to your students when their minds are open and speculative. They will need to imagine that they have the power to make things cleaner, quieter, sweeter, warmer, softer, and bigger than they are. The changes will make the world a better place in which to live. If the class has been confronted by current events that seem to overwhelm them (and everyone else), you'll have a wonderful opportunity to present this unit. Although it is based on wishful thinking, For a Better World ends by asking the students to consider which of their changes would most benefit the world and what would happen if such a change took place.

Administering the Unit

A few of the ways For a Better World might be used to develop multiple intelligences in your students are:

Developing the Interpersonal Intelligence

There is no guarantee that the students will be essentially altruistic in the changes they would like to make if they were magicians or good fairies. Their wishes could be selfish—the changes would simply make the world better for them. When they get to the last two prompts, however, they must consider which of their proposed changes would be best for the world. Accordingly, when discussing the activity with your students, you will want to emphasize this point and encourage them to think of how the greatest good could come to the greatest number of people. The child who is aware of issues concerning air quality, the availability and purity of drinking water, and

contamination of the soil and the seas will probably indicate the "clean" option as benefiting the world most.

Developing the Verbal-Linguistic Intelligence

The opportunity to express their ideas in words, whether spoken or written, is important for the intellectual and social development of your students. The child who is gifted in language will relish the challenge of putting his or her ideas into words that are appropriate and persuasive.

Developing the Naturalistic Intelligence

It is possible that the child who loves animals and the outdoors will express concern about what is happening to fish in contaminated waters or to species of plants and animals that are becoming extinct every day because people are encroaching on their habitats.

Following Through

If some of your students are fascinated by conditions in the world that should be changed and are capable of being changed, you can encourage them to gather facts and try to "prove" that the changes they have suggested would be of tremendous benefit to the world (or at least to their world). The subjects raised could well be of such magnitude that, for the purposes of further study, you may have to pare them down to sizes that your students can cope with (e.g., pollution of local streams, rivers, or lakes rather than of the oceans). If nothing else, however, this unit should make your students more aware of some problems that are of vital importance in their lives.

For a Better World

Let's pretend you are a magician or a good fairy. You want to make the world a better place.

What would you make clean that isn't clean? _____ What else?

_____

What would you make quiet? _____ Anything else?

_____

What would you make sweet? _____ Anything else?

_____

What would you make warm? _____ Anything else?

_____

What would you make soft? _____ Anything else?

_____

What would you make big? _____ What else?

_____

Which of these changes would do the most good for the world?

_____

_____

What would happen if you *could* make this change?

_____

_____

_____